The People of

LOWLAND
PERTHSHIRE

1600 - 1799

Carse of Gowrie
Strathearn
Western Strathmore

By

David Dobson

CLEARFIELD

Printed for Clearfield Company by
Genealogical Publishing Company
Baltimore, Maryland
2014

ISBN 978-0-8063-5679-2

Made in the United States of America

Contents

P. of THE NORTH PART of PERTH

P. of PERTH S.

BROADALBIN

Loch Tay

MOUNTAINS

THE STRATHERN

P. OF

MEN TEITH

P. of FIFE S.

The South Part of
PERTH SHIRE
Containing PERTH. STRAT-
HERN. STORMOUNT.
and CARS of GOURIE &c.

By H. Moll Geographer.

Miles of Great Britain

iv

The People of Lowland Perthshire, 1600-1799

INTRODUCTION

Perthshire, which lies in the center of Scotland, is intersected by a geological fault known as the Highland Line, which divides the Highlands from the Lowlands. The historical records, from the point of view of family historians, are generally more comprehensive for Lowland Scotland than for the Highlands, especially for parish records which are the backbone of Scottish genealogical research. As aids to genealogical research for those with roots in Perthshire The Clearfield Company has published two source books, firstly 'The People of Highland Perthshire', part of the 'Scottish Highlanders on the Eve of the Great Migration, 1725-1775' series, and secondly 'The People of Perth, 1600-1799' one of 'The People of the Scottish Burghs' series. This volume 'The People of Lowland Perthshire, 1600-1799' provides a source book covering the rest of the county.

Lowland Perthshire can be divided into three distinct regions all along river valleys. One section deals with the western part of Strathmore, the great valley in Gaelic, which stretches northeast from Perth. The emphasis is on the burghs of barony of Coupar Angus, Alyth, and Rattray, also the barony of Blairgowrie. As baronies were under the control of barons there were no burgesses, town councils, merchant or craft guilds, which normally provide documentary source material invaluable to the researcher. This section is therefore highly dependent on central government records, such as the Register of Deeds of the Court of Session, the Commissary Courts, family and estate papers as well as monumental inscriptions, largely located in the National Archives of Scotland in Edinburgh. To the south of

Strathmore and within the boundaries of Perthshire is the Carse of Gowrie which lies between the Sidlaw Hills and the River Tay. The Carse of Gowrie contains several villages including Errol, Inchture, Invergowrie, Longforgan, Leetown, Glencarse, St Madoes, and St Martins. Errol has the distinction of having the earliest parish records in Scotland, which date from 1553. In the medieval period the Carse, though fertile, was relatively under-populated and it was not until the Agricultural Revolution of the eighteenth century that the area was developed and settled. Early settlements were generally on the 'inch' [i.e. island] sites in the High Carse of Gowrie. The farmers used the Sidlaws as additional rough pasture for their animals. Farming improvements, especially drainage from about 1740, brought much land into production. The clay-built cottages of Leetown date from the early eighteenth century. Many farm buildings in the Carse date from about 1780. Linen manufacture, using local supplies of flax, was an important industry, for example Invergowrie grew as a bleachfield village. The references are predominantly from manuscript sources located in the National Archives of Scotland and from gravestone or monumental inscriptions. Strathearn is the broad river valley lying to the west of the city of Perth. The river Earn which runs through the valley joins the river Tay just east of Perth. It was once the center of a Pictish kingdom, and later a Celtic Earldom. Strathearn contains a number of small towns and villages including Abernethy, Auchterarder, Blackford, Braco, Bridge of Earn, Comrie, Crieff, Dunning, Forteviot, Methven and Muthill. This section is also largely based on documents found in archival sources. Major families or clans associated with Lowland Perthshire include Abernethy, Drummond, Graham, Gray, Haldane, Hay, Moncreiff, Murray, Oliphant, Ramsay, Rattray, and Rollo.

David Dobson

Dundee, Scotland

2014.

ADAM, ANDREW, [1656-1722], indweller in Thornebush, father of Peter, John, Margaret, Jean and Barbara. [Errol MI]

ADAM, PETER, born 1689, married, in Leyes, 1709. [HL#64]

ADAM, PETER, indweller in Errol 1739, died 1746, father of Isobel, Andrew, Margaret, John, Peter, Jean, Peter, and Patrick. [Errol MI] [NAS.CH2.887.7]

ADAMSON, JAMES, minister at Abernyte, 1782. [NAS.E326.1.102]

ALEXANDER, GEORGE, [1765-1817], farmer at East Bank. [Longforgan MI]

ALISON, ALEXANDER, [1737-1793], farmer in Cairy, wife Christian Morton [1747-1823]. [Kinfauns MI]

ANDERSON, EUPHAN, [1668-1731]. [Kilspindie MI]

ANDERSON, JAMES, and wife Janet Wighton, parents of John [1791-1800], Elizabeth [1780-1781], and Marjory [1778-1780]. [Longforgan MI]

ANTHONY, GILBERT, in Errol, 1682. [HL#1091]

ARLKEY, MARGARET, in Errol, 1744. [NAS.CH2.877.7.66]

AUCHENLECK, CHRISTIAN, an old infirm woman in Errol, 1739. [NAS.CH2.887.7]

AUCHTERLONIE, CHRISTIAN, relict of John Jackson of Muirhouse, now spouse to Gilbert Monurgund indweller there, 1682. [HL#1089]

BALFOUR, JAMES, schoolmaster at Errol, 1665, 1676. [HL#27/995]

BALLINGALL, WILLIAM, died 166-. [St Madoes MI]

BARNET, THOMAS, a weaver, wife Janet, children Janet died 1766, John and William died in infancy.[Kilspindie MI]

BARR, MAGDALENE, church seat rent, Inchture, 1772-1773. [NAS.CH2.188.1.291]

PEOPLE OF THE CARSE OF GOWRIE 1600-1799

BAXTER, PATRICK, [1662-1735], and his wife Janet Mitchell, [1672-1735], both died in Balgarvie. [Kilspindie MI]

BEARD, Mrs, in Errol, 1782. [NAS.E326.1.102]

BELL, WILLIAM, [1604-1665], minister in Auchtertool, Dron, and in Errol. [Errol MI]

BISSET, DAVID, farmer in Invergowrie, husband of Margaret Burns [1669-1724]. [Longforgan MI]

BLAIR, ALEXANDER, in Bandeen, wife Agnes Duncan [1591-1654], son William [1631-1662]. [Rossie MI]

BLAIR, FRANCIS, in Inchture, 1782. [NAS.E326.1.102]

BLAIR, KATHERINE, daughter and heir of the late James Blair of Newbigging, spouse of Peter Blair fiar of Leyes, 1662. [HL#44]

BLAIR, JAMES, eldest son to Robert Blair, a writer in Errol, 1741. [HL#86]

BLAIR, JOHN, minister at Kilspindie 1667 to 1691, husband of Helen Drummond, parents of John, Alexander, William, James, Helen, and Margaret. [F.IV.214]

BLAIR, ROBERT, a writer in Errol, 1742. [HL#88/89]

BLAIR, ROBERT, in Longforgan, 1782. [NAS.E326.1.102]

BLAIR, ROBERT, in Errol, 1782. [NAS.E326.1.102]

BLAIR, Sir THOMAS, the younger of Balthayock, purchased various lands and prporties in the parish of Errol in 1652. [RGS.X.58]

BLAIR, WILLIAM, of Kinfauns, 1654, 1662. [HL#2/44]

BOYD, JAMES, [1727-1786], wife Helen Smith, son James. [Longforgan MI]

BRODIE, GEORGE, in Errol, 1739. [NAS.CH2.887.7]

BROWN, ANNA, spouse of James Jackson, 1660, relict 1666. [HL#40/43]

BROWN, ELSPETH, an old woman in Errol, 1739. [NAS.CH2.887.7]

BROWN, GEORGE, at Aithmuir Mylne, 1654. [HL#957]

BROWN, Captain GEORGE, died at West Bank, 1797. [Longforgan MI]

BROWN, GEORGE, farm servant at Raws, husband of Jean Forester [1773-1807]. [Longforgan MI]

BROWN, JAMES, of Horn, 1671. [HL#14]

BROWN, JAMES, schoolmaster at Errol, 1692. [HL#1120]

BROWN, JAMES, at the Mill of Seggieden, father of George died 1712, and of William [1688-1743] who died at the Mill of Seggieden. [Kinfauns MI]

BROWN, JAMES, in Errol, 1739. [NAS.CH2.887.7]

BROWN, LAWRENCE, tenant farmer in Tippemuir, husband of Helen Donaldson [1742-1793]. [Kinfauns MI]

BROWN, PATRICK, in Waterybutts, and Margaret, daughter of the late James Jackson sometime in Polgavie, a marriage contract, 1703. [HL#58]

BROWN, WILLIAM, a farmer at West Bank, wife Elizabeth Stead died 179-. [Longforgan MI][NAS.E326.1.102]

BROWNHILLS, THOMAS, born 1725, a labourer in Kinnaird, Inchture, a Jacobite who was transported from Liverpool aboard the Veteran, master John Ricky, bound for the Leeward Islands on 5 May 1747, liberated by a French privateer and landed on Martinique in June 1747. [P.2.54][NA.SP36.102]

BRUCE, ALEXANDER, minister at Kinfauns 1611-1623. [F.IV.216]

BRUCE, ANDREW, in the East End of Errol before 1662. [RGS.XI.264]

BRUCE, JOHN, [1709-1781], in Chapelhill, wife Elspeth Hall, [1735-1801], son Archibald [1780-1822]. St Madoes MI]

BRUCE, ROBERT, [1766-1790], a weaver in Rait. [Kilspindie MI]

BRUCE, WILLIAM, of Fingask, husband of Janet Gibson [1614-1647]. [Rait MI]

PEOPLE OF THE CARSE OF GOWRIE 1600-1799

BRUCE, WILLIAM, shoemaker in Rait, husband of Katherine Lyall, a discharge, 1668. [HL#1010]

BUCHAN, JAMES, 63, Ann Buist, 65, children Margaret, Mary, Katherine, Elizabeth, Janet, James, David, and Robert a tailor in Errol, 1801. [St Madoes MI]

BUIST, GEORGE, in Inchyra, wife Catherine Millar, children Peter [1765-1769], and David [1766-1770]. [Kinfauns MI]

BUIST, JOHN, salmon fisher in Inchyra, wife Amelia Paterson [1710-1761]. [Kinfauns MI]

BUTCHART, ROBERT, [1694-1785], a mason in Kingoodie, wife Elizabeth Elder. [Longforgan MI]

BUTCHART, WILLIAM, church seat rent, Inchture, 1771-1773. [NAS.CH2.188.1.291]

CAMPSIE, JAMES, [1715-1775], tenant farmer in Kirk..., wife Margaret Buist. [St Madoes MI]

CAMSIE, JOHN, a miller in Kinfauns, father of John [1730-1741]. [Kinfauns MI]

CHALMERS, ARCHIBALD, [1766-1838], husband of Jean Hepburn [1762-1805]. [St Madoes MI]

CHALMERS, PETER, [1731-1796], farmer at Rayhill, wife Mary Easson [1742-1818]. [St Madoes MI]

CHAMBERS, JOHN, in Errol, 1662. [RGS.XI.265]

CHAPMAN, GEORGE, [1730-1795], minister at Kinfauns, wife Agnes Yeaman [1741-1808]. [Kinfauns MI] [NAS.E326.1.102]

CHRISTIE, CHARLES, [1721-1803, father of John in Inchyra. [St Madoes MI]

CHRISTIE, ISABEL, in Errol, 1744. [NAS.CH2.877.7.66]

CHRISTIE, JAMES, son of John Christie in Kilspindie, 1676. [HL#26]

CHRISTIE, PATRICK, in Kilspindie, 1673. [HL#21]

4 | P a g e

PEOPLE OF THE CARSE OF GOWRIE 1600-1799

CHRISTIE, ROBERT, from Errol, in the Royal Infirmary of Edinburgh, 1739. [NAS.CH2.887.7]

CHRYSTAL, HELEN, in Errol, died 1739. [NAS.CH2.887.7]

CHRISTLE, THOMAS, in Kinnaird, 1782.[NAS.E326.1.102]

CLARK, ALEXANDER, in Errol, 1782. [NAS.E326.1.102]

CLARK, JOHN, in Errol, 1782. [NAS.E326.1.102]

CLARK, WILLIAM, in Errol, 1782. [NAS.E326.1.102]

CLARK, Mrs, in Errol, 1782. [NAS.E326.1.102]

CLAYHILLS, JOHN, of Invergowrie, a contract, 1738. [HL#83]

CLUNIE, PATRICK, born 1649, married, in Leyes, 1709. [HL#64]

COB, ALEXANDER, born 1669, married, in Leyes, 1709. [HL#64]

COCK, PATRICK, in Balgay in the Carse, husband of Jean Jackson, a discharge, 1652. [HL#944]

CONSTABLE, PATRICK, in Inchture, 1782. [NAS.E326.1.102]

CONSTABLE, WILLIAM, died 1809. [Longforgan MI]

COUPAR, ALEXANDER, in Errol , 1739. [NAS.CH2.887.7]

COUPAR, JAMES, [1732-1805], a weaver, wife Elizabeth Lindsay [1732-1783], son James. [Kilspindie MI]

COUPAR, JAMES, church seat rent, Inchture, 1771-1773. [NAS.CH2.188.1.291]

COUPAR, JAMES, [1734-1800] at Kingoodie Quarry, wife Isabel Gellatly [1738-1816]. [Longforgan MI]

COUPAR, JOHN, minister at Kinfauns, ... [Kinfauns MI]

COUPAR, MATTHEW, minister at Kinfauns 1700 till his death on 13 February 1712, husband of Agnes Key, parents of John. [F.IV.216]

COUPAR, WILLIAM, died 1712, husband of Agnes Key. [Kinfauns MI]

5 | P a g e

COVENTRY, ROBERT, minister at Kilspindie 1727 to his death in 1761, father of David, Henrietta, Margaret, and Patrick. [F.IV.215]

COW, JANET, in Longforgan, 1715. [NAS.CH2/249/3]

CRAIGIE, JOHN, in Kinfauns, 1782. [NAS.E326.1.102]

CRAIGIE, ROBERT, President of the Court of Session, died 1760, buried at Greyfriars, Edinburgh. [Errol MI]

CRAIGOW, JOHN, in Abernyte, 1672. [HL#15]

CRAWFORD, HENRY, of Monorgan, 1709. [HL#65]

CRAWFORD JOHN, in Errol, 1782. [NAS.E326.1.102]

CRICHTON, WILLIAM, a hammerman in Kinfauns, husband of Anne Mathie [1716-1741]. [Kinfauns MI]

CUPAR, ANDREW, [1682-1732], in Rossie. [Rossie MI]

DAVIDSON, MARJORY, old,'whose daughter is a lunatick', in Errol, 1739. [NAS.CH2.887.7]

DAVIDSON, ROBERT, late of Balgay, a bond, 1737. [HL#82]

DEMPSTER, JOHN, [1651-1721], minister at St Madoes. [St Madoes MI]

DEWCAT, BARBARA, in Errol, deceased by 1655. [HL#961]

DOCTOR, JEAN, spouse of James Spence of Kilspindie, parents of Jean Spence spouse of Patrick Grant in Balgarvie, parents of James, John, Patrick, William and Jean Grant, and her great grandchild Jean Grant, daughter of David Grant, a glover in Perth, and to James, Ann, and Margaret Wright, her grandchildren, children of Laurence Wright, gardener in Carsegrange, and her daughter Catherine Spence, also to James, John, Patrick, and Laurence Arclay, her grandchildren, sons of the late Patrick Arclay in Pitmiddle, and her daughter Christian Spence, 1738. [HL#84]

DOIG, ROBERT, wright in Errol, 1771. [HL#911]

DONALD, FRANCIS, [1684-1750], died in Flacraig, wife Catherine Blair. [Kinnaird MI]

DONALD, JOHN, cordiner, died 1661, wife Magdalen Anderson. [Rait MI]

DONALDSON, JOHN, husband of Helen Brown [1683-1727]. [Kilspindie MI]

DORWARD, JAMES, [1774-1863], a shoemaker in Weston of Inchmartin, husband of Elspet Ker [1768-1850]. [Kinnaird MI]

DOW, ANTHONY, minister at Kilspindie 1789 to 1818, father of David and William. [F.IV.215]

DOW, WILLIAM, [1754-1826], died in Goddens. [Kinfauns MI]

DOW, Mrs, in Megginch, Errol, 1782. [NAS.E326.1.102]

DRUMMOND, PATRICK, 1767, and William Drummond, 1775. [Kinfauns MI]

DUFF, JOHN, a merchant in Errol, husband of Janet Grimont, parents of Mary [1730-1732]. [Errol MI]

DUNCAN, ANDREW, [1642-1722], wife Bathie Lownie, son Robert [1694-1757]. [Kilspindie MI]

DUNCAN, ANDREW, in Errol, 1744. [NAS.CH2.877.7.66]

DUNCAN, DAVID, indweller in Palmire, wife Elizabeth Liddle [1659-1717]. [Kilspindie MI]

DUNCAN, GEORGE, in Erroll, 1650. [HL#925/933]

DUNCAN, JAMES, son of Robert Duncan in the Motte of Errol, was granted the Templelands of Inchyra in 1654. [RGS.X.336]

DUNCAN, ROBERT, in Errol, 1691. [HL#68]

DUNCAN, ROBERT, [1694-1757], wife Jean Steel [1704-1761], sons David [1726-1804] and Andrew [1821-1813]. [Kilspindie MI]

DUNCAN, WILLIAM, a feuar in Errol, 1738. [HL#84]

DYKES, PATRICK, schoolmaster at Errol, 1680. [HL#1083]

PEOPLE OF THE CARSE OF GOWRIE 1600-1799

EASSON, AGNES, spouse to Andrew Clark a cotterman in Clashbenny, Errol, testament, 1607, Comm. St Andrews. [NAS]

EASSON, JAMES, in Inchture, 1782. [NAS.E326.1.102]

EASSON, THOMAS, in Inchcuning, Errol, testament, 1662, Comm. St Andrews. [NAS]

ELDER, ALEXANDER, [1687-1722], a farmer in Inchyra, wife Janet Miller [1691-1751], parents of Alexander a farmer in Pitcoag. [Kinfauns MI]

ELDER, ALEXANDER, in St Madoes, 1782. [NAS.E326.1.102]

ELDER, JOHN, a cottar in Monorgund, and his wife Catherine Gill, Longforgan, testament, 1616, Comm. St Andrews. [NAS]

ELDER, JOHN, and JANET, in Errol, 1739. [NAS.CH2.887.7]

ELDER, PATRICK, and wife Isobel Coupar in Longforgan, parents of Euphan [1723-1731]. [Longforgan MI]

ELLIS, ISOBEL, spouse to George Myretoun, in Westerton of Inchmartin, Errol, testament, 1618, Comm. St Andrews. [NAS]

ELLIS, JOHN, a cottar in Pitmidle, Kinnaird, testament, 1627, Comm. St Andrews. [NAS]

ELLIS, MARY, spouse to Gilbert Duncan in Errol, testament, 1713, Comm. St Andrews. [NAS]

FARQUHARSON, JEAN, at Dykeside of Megginch, Errol, testament, 1776, Comm. St Andrews. [NAS]

FENTON, DAVID, in Inchture, 1782. [NAS.E326.1.102]

FERGUSON, JAMES, boatman at Inchyra, Kinnoull, testament, 1675, Comm. St Andrews. [NAS]

FERRIER, GEORGE, a merchant in Errol, testament, 1787, Comm. St Andrews. [NAS]

8 | P a g e

FINLAY, PETER, [1760-1811], farmer at West Mains of Castle Huntly, wife Elizabeth Brown [1785-1819]. [Longforgan MI]

FINLAYSON, ISOBEL, sometime spouse to William Fyfe a cottar in Monorgund, testament, 1596, Comm. St Andrews. [NAS]

FINLAYSON, WILLIAM, smith at the east end of the Bridge of Tay, Kinnoull, testament, 1674, Comm. St Andrews. [NAS]

FLANNERS, JAMES, in Balgay, 1660. [HL#40]

FLEIGHT, PATRICK, died 1660, husband of Mareit Michel, in Kilspindie. [Kilspindie MI]

FLICHT, AGNES, spouse to James Fuird a cottarman in Rait, testament, 1613, Comm. St Andrews. [NAS]

FLEMING, JANET, in Longforgan, 1715. [NAS.CH2/249/3]

FLOWERS, JOHN, a smith in Longforgan, wife Margaret, parents of Elspeth died 1735. [Longforgan MI]

FLOWERS, JOHN, church seat rent, Inchture, 1772-1773. [NAS.CH2.188.1.291]

FOORD, JAMES, in Balthyock, Kinnoull, testament, 1673, Comm. St Andrews. [NAS]

FOORD, MARGARET, spouse to James Smith in Kinfauns, testament, 1673, Comm. St Andrews. [NAS]

FOORD, WILLIAM, in Greenside, Kilspindie, testament, 1748, Comm. St Andrews. [NAS]

FORBES, ELIZABETH, Lady Evelick, in Kilspindie, testament, 1683, Comm. St Andrews. [NAS]

FORBES, ROBERT, of Rossmyre, 1676. [HL#26]

FORRES, THOMAS, a mason in Longforgan, wife Isabella Matthew [1771-1800]. [Longforgan MI]

FORRESTER, DAVID, minister at Longforgan, testament, 1707, Comm. St Andrews. [NAS]

FOOTE, CHARLES, minister at Kinfauns 1732 to his death on 21 October 1758, husband of Barbara Stewart, parents of Ann, Robert, Barbara, and Euphan. [F.IV.217]

FOTHERINGHAM, GEORGE, of Bandeen, 1720. [HL#72]

FOTHERINGHAM, THOMAS, and his son John Fotheringham, were granted in life rent half of lands of Bandean, barony of Kinnoull, 1652. [RGS.X.56]

FOWLER, JAMES, minister at Kinfauns 1628 to his death in 1667, father of David, Thomas, and Elizabeth. [F.IV.216]

FREEMAN, ELSPET, spouse to John Gray a weaver in Cottarton of Muirton, Longforgan, testament, 1621, Comm. St Andrews. [NAS]

FUIRD, ANDREW, in Inchyra, Kinnoull, testament, 1636, Comm. St Andrews. [NAS]

FUIRD, JANET, spouse to Thomas Ford a cottar in Rait, testament, 1627, Comm. St Andrews. [NAS]

FUIRD, LUCRETIA, sometime spouse to John Duncan a tailor in Over Achmuir, Errol, testament, 1607, Comm. St Andrews. [NAS]

FUIRD, MARGARET, in Clein, Kinfauns, testament, 1607, Comm. St Andrews. [NAS]

FUTHIE, MARGARET, spouse to Andrew Black in Lochspout, Longforgan, testament, 1638, Comm. St Andrews. [NAS]

FYFE, AGNES, spouse to George Pittulloch in Unthank, Longforgan, testament, 1619, Comm. St Andrews. [NAS]

FYFE, GILBERT, in Longforgan, testament, 1635, Comm. St Andrews. [NAS]

FYFE, JAMES, [1610-1659], in Homes. [Longforgan MI]

FYFE, MARGARET, in Balcack, Errol, testament, 1613, Comm. St Andrews. [NAS]

FYFE, PATRICK, fiar of Dron, Longforgan, testament, 1624, Comm. St Andrews. [NAS]

FYFFE, WILLIAM, [1715-1747], husband of Margaret Millar in Polgavie, 1749. [Inchture MI]

FYFE, WILLIAM, [1756-1828]. [Kinnaird MI]

GAIRNS, ANDREW, in Errol, 1782. [NAS.E326.1.102]

GAIRNS, WILLIAM, husband of Magdalene Lyel, parents of Margaret [1763-1785]. [St Madoes MI]

GALL, JOHN, minister at Kinfauns 1687 to 1698, husband of Margaret Wemyss. [F.IV.216]

GALLOWAY, CHRISTIAN, relict of John Whyte in Kirkton of Errol, testament, 1621, Comm. St Andrews. [NAS]

GALLOWAY, HELEN, spouse to Archibald Logan in Errol, testament, 1617, Comm. St Andrews. [NAS]

GALLOWAY, JAMES, in Rait, testament, 1641, Comm. St Andrews. [NAS]

GALLOWAY, MARGARET, relict of Andrew Gourlay, sometime in Unthank, Longforgan, testament, 1673, Comm. St Andrews. [NAS]

GALLOWAY, PATRICK, a braboner in Rait, Kilspindie, testament, 1619, Comm. St Andrews. [NAS]

GALLOWAY, PATRICK, an indweller in Carse Grange, 1667. [HL#5]

GARDINER, ALEXANDER, in Errol, 1744. [NAS.CH2.877.7.66]

GARDINER, CHRISTINE, spouse to Andrew Tailor, in Clein, Kinfauns, testament, 1625, Comm. St Andrews. [NAS]

GARDINER, DAVID, [1714-1759]. [Kinfauns MI]

GARDINER, EDMOND, a cottar in Inchmartin, Errol, testament, 1596, Comm. St Andrews. [NAS]

GARDINER, GEORGE, in Errol, 1744. [NAS.CH2.877.7.66]

GARDINER, JOHN, in the Mains of Errol, testament, 1613, Comm. St Andrews. [NAS]

GARDINER, MARGARET, spouse to Patrick Gray in Muirie, Errol, testament, 1651, Comm. St Andrews. [NAS]

GARDINER, MARGARET, at the Bridgend of Tay, Kinnoull, testament, 1662, Comm. St Andrews. [NAS]

GARDINER, PATRICK, in Kilspindie, testament, 1649, Comm. St Andrews. [NAS]

GARDINER, PATRICK, in Orchard of Clein, Kinfauns, testament, 1699, Comm. St Andrews. [NAS]

GARDINER, THOMAS, in Errol, testament, 1599, Comm. St Andrews. [NAS]

GARDINER, THOMAS, in Pitmidle, Kinnaird, testament, 1682, Comm. St Andrews. [NAS]

GARDYNE, GEORGE, chamberlain to Inchture, 1652. [HL#944]

GARNER, WILLIAM, beadle of Errol, 1650s. [HL#928]

GARROW, PATRICK, in Balgavie, and his wife Christine Jackson, Inchture, testament, 1694, Comm. St Andrews. [NAS]

GEEKIE, PATRICK, [1737-1807], a farmer in Weembank and Flocklones, died at Balbunach. [Longforgan MI]

GENTLEMAN, WILLIAM, in Weston of Inchmartin, 1652. [HL#944]

GIBB, ANDREW, of Lochton, Longforgan, testament, 1684, Comm. St Andrews. [NAS]

GIBB, ANDREW, in Errol, 1739. [NAS.CH2.887.7]

GIBB, JANET, spouse to Gilbert Lowson, in Woodburnhead, Kinnaird, testament, 1613, Comm. St Andrews. [NAS]

GIBB, JANET, spouse to Thomas Gray in Littleton, Longforgan, testament, 1628, Comm. St Andrews. [NAS]

GIBB, ROBERT, a webster in Balgay, Invergowrie, testament, 1614, Comm. St Andrews. [NAS]

GIBB, ROBERT, in Lochton, Longforgan, testaments, 1619 & 1620, Comm. St Andrews. [NAS]

GIBB, ROBERT, the younger, of Lochton, Longforgan, testament, 1748, Comm. St Andrews. [NAS]

GIBB, WILLIAM, in Lungeis, Kilspindie, testament, 1700, Comm. St Andrews. [NAS]

GILL, CHARLES, in Errol, died 1739. [NAS.CH2.887.7]

GILL, JANET, spouse to John Hunter in Rait, Kilspindie, testament, 1621, Comm. St Andrews. [NAS]

GILL, WILLIAM, in Flacraig, Kinnaird, testament, 1651, Comm. St Andrews. [NAS]

GILLESPIE, CHRISTIAN, a widow in Errol, 1739. [NAS.CH2.887.7]

GOURLAY, JAMES, died 1642, wife Agnes Ogilvie. [Kinnaird MI]

GOURLAY, JOHN, farmer at Over-Kinfauns, Kinfauns, testament, 1799, Comm. St Andrews. [NAS]

GOURLAY, PATRICK, notary in Kinnaird, 1655/1657. [HL#3/961]

GOW, JANET, in Errol, 1744. [NAS.CH2.877.7.66]

GOW, JANET, an infirm woman in Errol, 1739. [NAS.CH2.887.7]

GOW, THOMAS, [1756-1826], in Chapelhill, wife May Sime [1754-1822], parents of James [1780-1795]. [St Madoes MI]

GOWAN, GEORGE, a cottar in Longforgan, testament, 1600, Comm. St Andrews. [NAS]

GOWANS, JOHN, in Longforgan, testament, 1625, Comm. St Andrews. [NAS]

GRAHAM, JAMES, of Monurgund, and his wife Margaret Gray, 1661. [RGS.XI.107]

GRAY, AGNES, sometime spouse of David Scott a brewster in Longforgan, testament, 1600, Comm. St Andrews. [NAS]

GRAY, ANDREW, in Bullion, Invergowrie, testament, 1616, Comm. St Andrews. [NAS]

GRAY, ANDREW, in Craigdealie, Kinnaird, testament, 1637, Comm. St Andrews. [NAS]

GRAY, ELIZABETH, Lady Balledgarno, Inchture, testament, 1745, Comm. St Andrews. [NAS]

GRAY, ELSPET, in Polgavie, Inchture, testament, 1637, Comm. St Andrews. [NAS]

GRAY, JAMES, in Errol, testament, 1651, Comm. St Andrews. [NAS]

GRAY, JOHN, in Bowhouse, Kilspindie, testament, 1641, Comm. St Andrews. [NAS]

GRAY, JOHN, of Baledgarno, Longforgan, testament, 1780, Comm. St Andrews. [NAS]

GRAY, MARJORIE, spouse to John Ogilvie in Longforgan, testament, 1617, Comm. St Andrews. [NAS]

GRAY, PATRICK, of Friendship Estate, Jamaica, [1746-1806], died in Glendoick House. [Kinfauns MI]

GRAY, ROBERT, husbandman in Longforgan, testament, 1596, Comm. St Andrews. [NAS]

GRAY, ROBERT, in Lochton, Longforgan, testament, 1628, Comm. St Andrews. [NAS]

GRAY, ROBERT, late tenant in Balledgarno, testament, 1747, Comm. St Andrews. [NAS]

GRAY, THOMAS, cottarman in Cotton of Blackness, Invergowrie, testament, 1598, Comm. St Andrews. [NAS]

GRAY, Mrs, in Longforgan, 1782. [NAS.E326.1.102]

GREEN, ALEXANDER, in Kilspindie, testament, 1750, Comm. St Andrews. [NAS]

GREEN, ELSPETH, an idiot in Errol, 1739. [NAS.CH2.887.7]

GREENHILL, PATRICK, in Errol, 1782. [NAS.E326.1.102]

GRIMMAN, or GRIMMOND, JOSEPH, [1710-1780], farmer at Pitrodie, Kilspindie, wife Elizabeth [1710-1795], children Janet [1732-1735], Katherine [1734-1739], Joseph [1744-1825], Jean [1753-1830, and William [1747-1814]. [Kilspindie MI]; testaments, 1784/1785, Comm. St Andrews. [NAS]

GRIMMAN, WILLIAM, [1677-1709], farmer in Kilspindie, wife Janet Hood [1668-1739], sons William [1691-1761] and Joseph [1710-1780]. [Kilspindie MI][HL#1112]

GUTHRIE, HENRY, minister at Kilspindie 1656 to 1665. [F.IV.214]

HACKNEY, HELEN, in Errol, 1744. [NAS.CH2.877.7.66]

HAGGART, JOHN, in Errol, 1739. [NAS.CH2.887.7]

HAITLIE, PATRICK, in Balgay, 1660. [HL#40]

HALDANE, JEAN, spouse to James Robertson in Balloch, Longforgan, testament, 1620, Comm. St Andrews. [NAS]

HALIBURTON, AGNES, spouse to Andrew Ogilvie in Balgay, Inchture, testament, 1624, Comm. St Andrews. [NAS]

HALIBURTON, THOMAS, minister at Errol, testament, 1651, Comm. St Andrews. [NAS]

HALL, ANDREW, a tailor in Longforgan, testament, 1649, Comm. St Andrews. [NAS]

HALL, ANDREW, beadle, husband of Grizel Waterson, parents of Jean [1752-1752] and Andrew [1759-1760]. [Kinfauns MI]

HALL, CATHERINE, spouse to William Malcolm in Errol, testament, 1662, Comm. St Andrews. [NAS]

HALL, JOHN, minister of Kilspindie 1646 to 1656, died January 1656, husband of .... Gray, parents of John and Andrew. [F.IV.214]

HALL, JOHN, [1633-1703, in Flawcraig, husband of Rachel Fyffe [1653-1714]. [Kinnaird MI]

HAMILTON, JOSEPH, schoolmaster at Errol, 1654. [HL#954]

HANNAY, MARGARET, spouse of James Anderson at the Mill of Monorgund, Longforgan, testament, 1627, Comm. St Andrews. [NAS]

HARDY, ANDREW, in Longforgan, 1715. [NAS.CH2/249/3]

HAY, Mrs ANN, third daughter of the late Peter Hay of Leyes, Errol, testament, 1705, Comm. St Andrews. [NAS]

HAY, GEORGE, of Leyes, son and heir to Peter Hay of Leyes, 1712, 1713, 1728. [HL#70/71/77]; testaments, 1752/1753, Comm. St Andrews. [NAS]

HAY, HELEN, spouse to Thomas Trumbull of Bogmill, Errol, testament, 1662, Comm. St Andrews. [NAS]

HAY, JAMES, of Seggieden, Kinfauns, testament, 1781, Comm. St Andrews. [NAS]

HAY, JOHN, brother-german of Peter Hay of Leyes, Errol, testament, 1692, Comm. St Andrews. [NAS]

HAY, Sir JOHN, of Murie, Errol, testament, 1704, Comm. St Andrews. [NAS]

HAY, JOHN, of Pitfour, and his third son Francis Hay and his third son Edward Hay, bonds, 1733. [HL#79]

HAY, MARGARET, spouse to Patrick Kynnard in Inchmichael, Errol, testament, 1618, Comm. St Andrews. [NAS]

HAY, PATRICK, feuar of Leyes, 1692. [HL#29/69]

HAY, PETER, son and heir of the late Peter Hay of Kilspindie, 1617. [HL#35]

HAY, PETER, of Megginch, Errol, testament, 1617, Comm. St Andrews. [NAS]

HAY, PETER, in Carles Oxgate, Errol, 1662. [RGS.XI.264]

HAY, PETER, fiar of Leyes, husband of Kathleen Blair, parents of John, George, James, Katherine, and Anna, 1680, 1694, 1696, 1701, 1705. [HL#46/51/52/53/55/56]; testament, 1713, Comm. St Andrews. [NAS]

HAY, WILLIAM, son of the late Peter Hay, at the Mill of Auchmuir, Errol, testament, 1620, Comm. St Andrews. [NAS]

HAY, Mrs, in Kinfauns, 1782. [NAS.E326.1.102]

HEN, GILBERT, in Monurgund, Longforgan, testament, 1626, Comm. St Andrews. [NAS]

HENDERSON, ANDREW, in Weston of Inchleslie, Errol, testament, 1685, Comm. St Andrews. [NAS]

HENDERSON, PATRICK, in Kirkton of Errol, testament, 1599, Comm. St Andrews. [NAS]

HENDERSON, PATRICK, in Belseis, Errol, testament, 1619, Comm. St Andrews. [NAS]

HEPBURN, JAMES, the younger, in Errol, a witness, 1726. [HL#750]

HEPBURN, NINIAN, in Errol, testament, 1626, Comm. St Andrews. [NAS]

HEPBURN, WILLIAM, in Errol, a witness, 1726. [HL#750]

HERAULL, ANDREW, in Littleton, Longforgan, testament, 1681, Comm. St Andrews. [NAS]

HERON, THOMAS, in Boghall, St Martins, testament, 1685, Comm. St Andrews. [NAS]

HERRING, MARGARET, spouse to Andrew Thomson a cottarman in Cotton of Blackness, Invergowrie, testament, 1607, Comm. St Andrews. [NAS]

HILL, JANET, in Cotton of Newbigging, Invergowrie, testament, 1607, Comm. St Andrews. [NAS]

HILL, JOHN, the elder, in Inchmichael, and his wife Agnes Hunter, Errol, testament, 1773, Comm. St Andrews. [NAS]

HILL, PATRICK, in Errol, 1782. [NAS.E326.1.102]

HILL, ROBERT, tenant farmer in Inchmichael, husband of Katherine Mitchell, parents of Margaret -1748-1752]. [Errol MI]; testament, 1771, Comm. St Andrews. [NAS]

HOBBIE, or FLEDGEOUR, ROBERT, in Longforgan, testament, 1616, Comm. St Andrews. [NAS]

HOG, ELSPETH, a widow with two children in Errol, 1739, 1744. [NAS.CH2.887.7]

HONEY, PATRICK, in Gaskhill of Kinnoull, son of the late James Honey in Gairdrum, Kinnoull, testament, 1719, Comm. St Andrews. [NAS]

HOOD, JAMES, in Craigdale or Craigdeallie, Kinnaird, wife Isabel Gourlay [1594-1664], Rossie MI., testament, 1649, Comm. St Andrews. [NAS]

HOOD, JOHN, in Burnside of Kinfauns, testament, 1673, Comm. St Andrews. [NAS]

HOOD, JOHN, husband of Janet Cram [1748-1810]. [Kinfauns MI]

HOOD, ROBERT, a tenant in Inchleslie, testament, 1717, Comm. St Andrews. [NAS]

HOOD, ROBERT, a tenant in Balgay, Inchture, testaments, 1777/1778, Comm. St Andrews. [NAS]

HOWIE, ALEXANDER, in Byres, St Martin's, testament, 1714, Comm. St Andrews. [NAS]

HUME, JOHN, [1728-1802], wife Christine Barclay [1729-1803]. [Longforgan MI]

HUME, JOHN, [1770-1815], a brewer and baker in Longforgan. [Longforgan MI]

HUNTER, ELIZABETH, spouse to George Moodie in Moncur, Inchture, testament, 1681, Comm. St Andrews. [NAS]

HUNTER, GEORGE, in Carnie [1707-1775], wife Isabel Miller, parents of Patrick died 1778. [St Madoes MI]

HUNTER, HELEN, spouse to Andrew Hunter in Inchmichael, Errol, testament, 1685, Comm. St Andrews. [NAS]

HUNTER, JAMES, died 1662. [Kilspindie MI]

HUNTER, JAMES, in Errol, 1782. [NAS.E326.1.102]

HUNTER, JOHN, in Craighall, Errol, testament, 1599, Comm. St Andrews. [NAS]

HUNTER, JOHN, late servant to Mrs Agnes Hunter in Haughmuir, Errol, testament, 1771, Comm. St Andrews. [NAS]

HUNTER, PATRICK, in Errol, testament, 1715, Comm. St Andrews. [NAS]

HUNTER, PATRICK, in Abernyte, and Janet Coupar in Longforgan, wedding banns 9 January 1716. [NAS.CH2/249/3]

HUNTER, PATRICK, in Abernyte, 1782. [NAS.E326.1.102]

HUNTER, THOMAS, in Inchture, 1782. [NAS.E326.1.102]

HUNTER, WILLIAM, of Pitlowie, Kinfauns, testament, 1639, Comm. St Andrews. [NAS]

HUNTER, WILLIAM, a weaver in Inchmichael, Errol, testament, 1775, Comm. St Andrews. [NAS]

HUNTER,......, in Longforgan, 1782. [NAS.E326.1.102]

HUTCHEON, HENRY, in Durrage, Kilspindie, testament, 1641, Comm. St Andrews. [NAS]

HUTTON, DAVID, at the Mill of Inchmichael, Errol, testament, 1620, Comm. St Andrews. [NAS]

HUTTON, EUPHAN, in Errol, 1744. [NAS.CH2.877.7.66]

HUTTON, JAMES, in Inchmichael, brother german of Patrick Hutton in Milne of Aithmuir, 1685. [HL#1101]

HUTTON, JOHN, at the Mill of Auchnure, Errol, testament, 1685, Comm. St Andrews. [NAS]

HUTTON, PATRICK, pickieman at the Milne of Aithmuir, 1685. [HL#1101]

IMRIE, ANDREW, [1724-1776] a smith, died in Glendoick. [Kinfauns MI]

INGLIS, ROBERT, wife Agnes Doinet, in Glendoick, daughter Agnes [1746-1758]. [Kilspindie MI]

INGLIS, WILLIAM, minister at Kilspindie 1698 to his death in 1727, husband of (1) Christian Mitchell, (2) Janet Gordon. [F.IV.215]

IRELAND, JOHN, [1754-1820], miller in Inchyra, husband of Elspeth Gairns, 1762-1840]. [St Madoes MI]

ISLES, ALEXANDER, [1692-1742], tenant farmer in Weston of Inchkinning. [Errol MI]

ISLES, WILLIAM, [1688-1744], a shoemaker, wife Helen Clark [1695-1730]. [Errol MI]

JACK, AGNES, spouse to William Rollok in Nether Durie, Kilspindie, testament, 1650, Comm. St Andrews. [NAS]

JACK, ANDREW, wife Janet Blair, in Rossie, sons Robert and Andrew, 1661. [Rossie MI]

JACK, ANDREW, in Milnhill, Longforgan, testament, 1723, Comm. St Andrews. [NAS]

JACK, or KIDD, ELSPET, spouse to the late Walter Skirling in Trufilis, Kilspindie, testament, 1600, Comm. St Andrews. [NAS]

JACK, JAMES, in Rossie, spouse Janet Gray [1629-1657]. [Rossie MI]

JACK, ROBERT, in Abernyte, 1672. [HL#15]

JACK, ROBERT, a weaver in West Inchmartin, husband of Isabel Steel, [1749-1792]. [Kilspindie MI]

JACKSON, BESSIE, spouse to Robert Jackson in Carsegrange, Errol, testament, 1618, Comm. St Andrews. [NAS]

JACKSON, CHRISTIAN, in Rait, spouse to John Gaw a husbandman there, testament, 1598, Comm. St Andrews. [NAS]

JACKSON, DAVID, son of Edmund Jackson in Errol, 1681. [HL#1084]

JACKSON, EDMOND, spouse to Catharine Smyth, in Kilspindie, testament, 1636, Comm. St Andrews. [NAS]

JACKSON, ELIZABETH, sometime spouse to Edmond Jackson in Auchmuir, testament, 1615, Comm. St Andrews. [NAS]

JACKSON, EDMOND, in Errol, 1662. [RGS.XI.265]

JACKSON, GILBERT, portioner of Carsegrange, 1657, 1664. [HL#3/4]

JACKSON, GILBERT, a merchant in Errol, 1681, a discharge. [HL#1084]

JACKSON, HELEN, daughter of James Jackson of Waterybutts, a marriage contract, 1660. [HL#40]

JACKSON, HENRY, son of Robert Jackson in Inchmartin, Errol, testament, 1599, Comm. St Andrews. [NAS]

JACKSON, HENRY, a workman in Mangalelands, Inchture, testament, 1778, Comm. St Andrews. [NAS]

JACKSON, ISOBEL, in Polgavie, Inchture, testament, 1618, Comm. St Andrews. [NAS]

JACKSON, JAMES, at the Brig of Carsegrange, Errol, testament, 1596, Comm. St Andrews. [NAS]

JACKSON, JAMES, sometime of Waterybutts. 1671. [HL#14]

JACKSON, JANET, relict of Robert Syme in Auchmuir, testament, 1598, Comm. St Andrews. [NAS]

JACKSON, JANET, in Errol, 1739. [NAS.CH2.887.7]

JACKSON, JOHN, portioner of Polgavie, Inchture, testament, 1620, Comm. St Andrews. [NAS]

JACKSON, JOHN, of Muirhouses, 1670. [HL#10]

JACKSON, JOHN, [1740-1823], a farmer, wife Jean Archer [1765-1845]. [Longforgan MI]

JACKSON, PATRICK, in Inchture, 1657, marriage contact with Helen Jackson, 1660, 1666. [HL#6/7/8/40/43]

JACKSON, PATRICK, in Longforgan, 1673. [HL#20]

JACKSON, ROBERT, church seat rent, Inchture, 177-1773. [NAS.CH2.188.1.291]

JACKSON, THOMAS, [1756-1827], wife Margaret Grimman [1762-1838]. [Kilspindie MI]

JACKSON, WILLIAM, indweller in Errol, 1728. [HL#77]; an old and poor brother to John Jackson in Carse Grange, 1739. [NAS.CH2.887.7]

JOBSON, JAMES, in Errol, 1782. [NAS.E326.1.102]

KETHEL, JOHN, a witness in Errol, 1741. [HL#86]

KEYL, JAMES, in Longforgan, 1782. [NAS.E326.1.102]

KIDD, JOHN, [1747-1805]. [Longforgan MI]

KIELL, JAMES, [1733-1803], farmer at the Mill of Monorgan, wife Elizabeth Blair [1749-1809]. [Longforgan MI]

KIELL, PETER, [1729-1810], farmer at Raws, Monorgan, wife Marjory Smith [1741-1833] at West Pilmore. [Longforgan MI]

KIELL, PETER, died 1789. [Longforgan MI]

KININMONTH, JAMES, [1663-1732], wife Margaret Smith [1672-1736]. [Rossie MI]

KININMONT, PATRICK, and spouse Euphan Grizell, in Baledgarno, parents of William [1741-1745], Robert [1742-1745], Robert [1742-1745], and William [1748-1748]. [Inchture MI]

KINMAND, JOHN, in Errol, 1782. [NAS.E326.1.102]

KINMAN, PATRICK, in Inchture, 1782. [NAS.E326.1.102]

KINNEIR, CHARLES, in Errol, 1782. [NAS.E326.1.102]

KINTRE, WILLIAM, husband of Margaret Murdoch [1682-1732]. [Kilspindie MI]

LYON, ROBERT, minister at Kinfauns 1714 until his death on 1 August 1730, husband of Jean Dalgleish, parents of William, Joan, Barbara, Isobel, Margaret, and Catherine. [F.IV.216]

LAIRD, JAMES, wife Isabel Paterson, in Pitmidel, parents of Margaret, Margaret, Isobel, Elspet, Isobel, Elisabeth, and May, 1743. [Kinnaird MI]

LAIRD, THOMAS, a farmer at Gardswell, wife Janet Boyd, parents od Margaret [1765-1769] and James died 1826. [Kinnaird MI]

LAUDER, WILLIAM, tenant farmer in Glencarse, 1771. [HL#911]

LAUTHER, Mrs, in Kinfauns, 1782. [NAS.E326.1.102]

LAYELL, GILBERT, [1730-1785], a fisher, died in Ribney, father of John. [St Madoes MI]

LINDSAY, ALEXANDER, in Kilspindie, eldest son of Alexander Lindsay and his first wife Margaret Falconer, father of William Lindsay, 1657. [RGS.X.615]

LINDSAY, WILLIAM, of Kilspindie, deceased by 1657, eldest son of Alexander Lindsay of Evelick and his second wife Elizabeth Forbes. [RGS.X.615]

LINDSAY, WILLIAM, of Kilspindie, later of Carse Grange, 1672, 1673, 1676. [HL#16/18/21/22/26/27/28/31]

LOBAN, ALEXANDER, [1711- 1784]. [Inchture MI]

LOGAN, ALEXANDER, [1723-1802]. [Longforgan MI]

LORIMER, ISABEL, in Errol, 1744. [NAS.CH2.877.7.66]

LOW, ANN, in Errol, died 1739. [NAS.CH2.887.7]

LOWDEN, MARY, in Errol, 1744. [NAS.CH2.877.7.66]

LUNAN, EUPHAN, in Longforgan, 1715. [NAS.CH2/249/3]

LYON, GEORGE, minister in Longforgan, 1782. [NAS.E326.1.102]

MCCULLIE, ANDREW, a tailor in Rait, husband of Elizabeth Reid, 17... [Kilspindie MI]

MCCULLIE, GEORGE, tenant farmer in Flawcraigs, died 1782, wife Mary Spalding, died 1787. [Kilspindie MI]

MCDOUGAL, ALEXANDER, in Kilspindie, 1782. [NAS.E326.1.102]

MCDOUGAL, DANIEL, [1761-1796], gardener at Megginch Castle. [Errol MI]

MACGRUTHER, GEORGE, son of the deceased James MacGruther in Newmiln, 1676. [HL#25]

MCINNES, WILLIAM, servant to George Hay of Leyes, 1728. [HL#77]

MCINROY, DUNCAN, [1766-1827], wife Euphemia Robertson, [1781-1878]. [Errol MI]

MCINTOSH, ALEXANDER, officer in Errol, 1728. [HL#77]

MACKAY, MARGARET, an old woman in Errol, 1739. [NAS.CH2.887.7]

MCLACHLAN, CHARLES, [1765-1804], wife Margaret McCullooch. [Longforgan MI]

MCLAGAN, GEORGE, [1704-1784]. husband of (1) Catherine Davie [1700-1763], (2) Isabel Bryson. [Kilspindie MI]

MARSHAL, GEORGE, an old man in Errol, 1739. [NAS.CH2.887.7]

MARTIN, CHRISTINE, in Errol, 1744. [NAS.CH2.877.7.66]

MARTIN, EUPHAN, in Errol, 1739, 1744. [NAS.CH2.887.7]

MARTIN, ISABEL, an orphan in Errol, 1739. [NAS.CH2.887.7]

MARTIN, MARGARET, bedridden in Errol, 1739. [NAS.CH2.887.7]

MATHERS, JAMES, smith in Evlick, husband of Beatrice Arklay [1684-1730], son James [1714-1720]. [Kilspindie MI]

MATHERS, WILLIAM, [1841-1815], farmer on Castle Huntly estate, wife Margaret Salmon. [Longforgan MI]

MATHESON, FRANCIS, [1702-1732], a wright in Longforgan, spouse of Elizabeth, parents of John, a wright in Longforgan, and Janet. [Inchture MI]

MATTHEW, JAMES, in Errol, 1782. [NAS.E326.1.102]

MATTHEW, JOHN, in Errol, 1782. [NAS.E326.1.102]

MATTHEW, PATRICK, in Errol, 1782. [NAS.E326.1.102]

MATTHEW, THOMAS, in Errol, 1782. [NAS.E326.1.102]

MATTHEWSON, GEORGE, in Inchture, 1782. [NAS.E326.1.102]

MATHIE, JOHN, a cooper in Inchyra, husband of Anne Runciman, parents of Anne [1716-1741] and Robert . [Kinfauns MI]

MATHIE, ROBERT, husband of Ellen Duncan [1715-1772]. [Kinfauns MI]

MATTHEW, ISABEL, a widow with two children in Errol, 1739. [NAS.CH2.887.7]

MATTHEW, ISABEL, an old unmarried woman in Errol, 1739. [NAS.CH2.887.7]

MATTHEW, JAMES, [1751-1828], a wright in Longforgan. [Longforgan MI]

MATTHEW, MARJORY, an old woman in Errol, 1739. [NAS.CH2.887.7]

MATTHEW, THOMAS, in Balgay, 1660. [HL#40]

MATTHEW, THOMAS, in Longforgan, 1782. [NAS.E326.1.102]

MAXWELL, GEORGE, husband of Janet Fyfe [1580-1652]. [Longforgan MI]

MERCER, KATHERINE, spouse of Robert Butcher, buried in Longforgan, 1715. [NAS.CH2/249/3]

MILL, Reverend JAMES, in Kinnaird, 1782. [NAS.E326.1.102]

MILL, THOMAS, in Longforgan, 1782. [NAS.E326.1.102]

MILLAR, ANDREW, [1648-1732], wife Agnes Stewart [died 1730]. [Rossie MI]

MILLAR, FARQUHAR, servant to George Hay of Leyes, 1728. [HL#77]

MILLAR, GEORGE, in Windyedge, 1673. [HL#21]

MILLAR, GEORGE, a farmer in Mill of Godens, died 1712, wife Anna Blair [1664-1731], son George [1700-1768]. [Kilspindie MI]

MILLAR, GEORGE, [1700-1768], farmer in Mill of Godens, wife Elizabeth Couper [1715-1766], son George [1736-1812]. [Kilspindie MI]

MILLAR, GEORGE, [1736-1812], farmer in Mill of Godens, wife Elizabeth Coupar [1754-1826]. [Kilspindie MI]

MILLAR, GEORGE, minister of Inchture, 1782. [NAS.E326.1.102]

MILLER, JAMES, [1678-1725], wife Elizabeth Ducat [1680-1740]. [Kilspindie MI]

MILLER, JOHN, [1666-1737], wife Isabel Davidson. [Rait MI]

MILLAR, JOHN, [1733-1799], minister at Inchture. [Inchture MI]

MILLER, PATRICK, [1704-1758], tenant farmer in Nether Durlef, husband of Margaret Gardner [1720-1797], daughter Margaret [1744-1785]. [Rait MI]

MILLER, ROBERT, in Inchture, 1782. [NAS.E326.1.102]

MITCHELL, PATRICK, tenant in Inchture, son in law of Patrick Hutton and his wife Elspet Galloway, 1742. [HL#88]

MITCHELL, THOMAS, minister at Abernyte, and his servant Jean Mitchell, 1728. [NAS.CH1/2/57/1-77]

MONCREIFF, HELEN, relict of William Bell minister at Errol, a discharge, 1666. [HL#1000]

MONCUR, PATRICK, in the Temple lands of Bandean, barony of Kinnoull, 1652. [RGS.X.56]

MONORGUN, JAMES, in Seasyde, 1681. [HL#1085]

MONORGUND, GILBERT, of that Ilk, husband of Katherine Campbell, and their eldest son James Monurgund, a sasine, 1643. [NAS.RS1.53.584]

MORRIS, JAMES, church seat rent, Inchture, 1772-1773. [NAS.CH2.188.1.291]

MORTON, ANDREW, tenant famer in the Mains of Errol, 1771. [HL#911]; in Errol, 1782. [NAS.E326.1.102]

MUDIE, WILLIAM, [1607-1659], in Polgavie. [Inchture MI]

MURRAY, JOHN, minister at Kinfauns 1667 to his death on 18 January 1687, husband of Anna Ramsay. [F.IV.216]

MURRAY, JOHN, a weaver in Longforgan, died 1803, wife Janet Gardiner [1755-1834] a midwife. [Longforgan MI]

MYLES, GEORGE, husband of Christian Brugh, parents of John [1768-1788]. [Kinfauns MI]

NAESMITH, WILLIAM, gardener to the Earl of Northesk, and spouse Isobel Bruce, at the Moat of Erroll, 1688. [HL#49]

NAIRN, SAMUEL, minister at Erroll, 1703. [NAS.CH1.2..4.fos.295-296]

NICOL, JAMES, tenant in Homes, died 1741, spouse Helen Davie. [Inchture MI]

NICOLSON, JOHN, parson of Errol, 1683. [HL#1034]

OGILVIE, ANDREW, in Balgay, 1657, 1664. [HL#3/4]

OGILVIE, ELIZABETH, daughter of the late Andrew Ogilvie sometime in Balgay, 1678. [HL#45]

OGILVIE, Sir PATRICK, of Inchmartin, and his son William Ogilvie, a sasine, 1643. [NAS.RS1.53.584]; Sir Patrick died by 1652. [RGS.X.56]

OGILVIE, PATRICK, portioner of Carse Grange, dead by 1676, spouse of Anna Jackson,1671, 1672, 1673. [HL#13/15/16/17/21/22/23/24/25/26/40]

OGILVIE, PATRICK, a notary in Carsegrange, 1670. [HL#1020]

OGILVIE, PATRICK, and his wife Elizabeth Ogilvie, in the lands of Templehall and Broomhall, parish of Longforgan, a bond, 1696. [NAS.RD4.79]

OGILVIE, THOMAS, in the barony of Longforgan, a sasine, 1650. [NAS.RS51.1]

OGILVIE, THOMAS, a farmer in Kilspindie, husband of Jean Paterson [1741-1782]. [Kinnaird MI]

OGILVIE, WILLIAM, of Murie, was granted the lands of the Mains of Errol in 1652. [RGS.X.57]

OLIPHANT, JOHN, in Inchture, spouse Catherine Low [1759-1819], children John [1788-1789], and Robert [1779-1786]. [Inchture MI]

OMAY, ALEXANDER, [1573-1639], a preacher in Monydie and in Errol. [Errol MI]

PATERSON, ALEXANDER, and wife Margaret Christalm parents of Robert [1750-1750]. [Kinfauns MI]

PATERSON, ANDREW, a flesher in the Temple lands of Bandean, barony of Kinnoull, 1652. [RGS.X.56]

PATERSON, ANDREW, tenant farmer in Hole of Glencarse, husband of Margaret Alison [1683-1750]. [Kinfauns MI]

PATERSON, GEORGE, in Longforgan, 1782. [NAS.E326.1.102]

PATERSON, WILLIAM, husband of Beatrice Moor, parents of Richard [1740-1747] who died in Pitmiddie. [Kinnaird MI]

PATILLO, CHARLES, [1747-1818], farmer in Haughead, husband of Katherine Forgan. [St Madoes MI]

PEEBLES, JAMES, spouse Janet Alexander died 1699. [Inchture MI]

PEEBLES, JAMES, draper in Inchture, spouse Ann Miller [1718-1778], parents of Mary, James, and William [1753-1826]. [Inchture MI]

PEIRY, DAVID, was rebuked before the congregation of Longforgan church, 1715. [NAS.CH2/249/3]

PENDER, ROBERT, a flesher in St Madoes, husband of Elspet Pattison [1708-1774], parents of Mary. [St Madoes MI]

PERSON, PATRICK, [1700-1730]. [Rossie MI]

PERT, ALEXANDER, [1590-1646]. [Kinfauns MI]

PILLER, JOHN, in Mill of Heugh, wife Sarah Miller [1676-1757]. [Errol MI]

PIRIE, ROBERT, in Errol, 1739. [NAS.CH2.887.7]

PITKETHLY, THOMAS, in Errol, 1739. [NAS.CH2.887.7]

PITTILLOCK, JEAN, an old infirm woman in Errol, 1739. [NAS.CH2.887.7]

PITTILLOCK, MARY, in Errol, 1744. [NAS.CH2.877.7.66]

PLAYFAIR, GEORGE, in Errol, 1662. [RGS.XI.265]

PLAYFAIR, PETER, in Aithmuir, 1654. [HL#957]

POWRIE, ANDREW, [1697-1789], a farmer, wife Janet White [1710-1783]. [Rait MI]

POWRIE, JOHN, in Mains of Erroll, 1670, 1710. [HL#67/1020]

POWRIE, JANET, eldest daughter of John Powrie in Mains of Errol, spouse of William Whitehead, 1710. [HL#67/68]

PRAIN, ALEXANDER, [1766-1817], a manufacturer in Longforgan, wife Isabel Coupar [1760-1843]. [Longforgan MI]

RANDALL, THOMAS, minister at Inchture, 1742. [HL#88]

RANKEN, THOMAS, and his wife Euphan Young, in Cotton, parents of Janet [1717-1730]. [Inchture MI]

RATTRAY, DAVID, in Errol, 1782. [NAS.E326.1.102]

RATTRAY, JAMES, a writer in Errol, 1742. [HL#89]

RAE, ALEXANDER, and spouse Elizabeth Matthew [1743-1796], at Millhill. [Inchture MI]

RATTRAY, JOHN, church seat rent, Inchture, 1771-1773. [NAS.CH2.188.1.291]

RENNIE, JANET, in Longforgan, 1715. [NAS.CH2/249/3]

RICHARDSON, WILLIAM, in Longforgan, 1715. [NAS.CH2/249/3]

ROBERTSON, ANDREW, in the Temple lands of Bandean, barony of Kinnoull, 1652. [RGS.X.56]

ROBERTSON, GILBERT, an indweller in Carse Grange, 1667. [HL#5]

ROBERTSON, JAMES, a tenant in South Leyes, 1709. [HL#64]

ROBERTSON, JEAN, in Errol, 1739. [NAS.CH2.887.7]

ROBERTSON, JOHN, a tenant in Wester Leyes, 1709. [HL#64]

ROBERTSON, JOSEPH, church seat rent, Inchture, 1771-1773. [NAS.CH2.188.1.291]

ROBERTSON, MARGARET, in Errol, 1744. [NAS.CH2.877.7.66]

ROBERTSON, PATRICK, farmer in Pitartie, father of William [1705-1725]. [Kilspindie MI]

RODGER, ALEXANDER, [1735-1780], miller in Monorgan, wife Janet Reid, [1729-1785], parents of Henry, James and Peter. [Longforgan MI]

ROGER, ALEXANDER, a weaver in Clean, father of John [1720-1721]. [Kinfauns MI]

ROGERS, ALEXANDER, a wright in Glendoick, wife Isabel Millar [1732-1776], children Ann [1751-1752] and David. [Kinfauns MI]

SCOBBIE, MARGARET, an inform woman in Errol, 1739. [NAS.CH2.887.7]

SELLAR, JAMES, a brewer in Errol, 1681. [HL#1088]

SHARP, ROBERT, [1709-1747], wife Jean McLagan [1710-1773], son Robert. [Kilspindie MI]

SHARP, THOMAS, husband of Jean Gray [1721-1783]. Daughter Elizabeth [1761-1777]. [Kilspindie MI]

SHARP, WILLIAM, a weaver in Teuchievard, father of John [1705-1723] a weaver. [Kinfauns MI]

SIM, DAVID, tenant farmer of the Mains of Errol before 1771. [HL#911]

SIM, ELIZABETH, in Errol, 1782. [NAS.E326.1.102]

SIM, JAMES, in Errol, 1782. [NAS.E326.1.102]

SIM, MARGARET, in Errol, 1744. [NAS.CH2.877.7.66]

SIMSON, WILLIAM, in Longforgan, 1715. [NAS.CH2/249/3]

SMALL, ANDREW, tenant in Carnie, wife Ann Miller, parents of Peter [1781-1781], Margaret, Andrew, Cicily, Ann, John, Elizabeth, James, William [1796-1802], Isabel and David. [St Madoes MI]

SMITH, ALEXANDER, sometime tenant in Weston of Inchmartin, and his relict Isobel Blair, 1741. [HL#86]

SMITH, ANDREW, [1578-1646], a farmer in Balindean, husband of Agnes Cuthbert, parents of William [1614-1691]. [Rossie MI]

SMITH, ANDREW, [1667-1731], wife Magdalen Blair [1680-1758], parents of John, William, Ann, and Andrew. [Rossie MI]

SMITH, DAVID, [1753-1808]. [Kinfauns MI]

SMITH, GEORGE, in Longforgan, 1715. [NAS.CH2/249/3]

SMITH, JAMES, [1750-1813], wife Jean Nicol [1764-1821]. [Longforgan MI] [NAS.E326.1.102]

SMITH, JAMES, and Helen Young, in Myreside of Forgan, 1761. [Longforgan MI]

SMITH, JOHN, an old man in Errol, 1739. [NAS.CH2.887.7]

SMITH, JOHN, in Cotton, husband of Margaret Whittet, parents of Barbara [1782-1786]. [St Madoes MI]

SMITH, MARGARET, eldest daughter to the late Alexander Smith sometime tenant in Wester Inchmartin and his spouse Isobel Blair, 1742. [HL#89]

SMITH, PATRICK, a poor weaver whose wife has lost her judgement, in Errol, 1739. [NAS.CH2.887.7]

SOUTER, JAMES, [1729-1800], tenant farmer in Craigdellie, wife Margaret Black [1734-1814]. [Kinnaird MI]

SOUTAR, KATHERINE, in Errol, 1739. [NAS.CH2.887.7]

SPALDING, JOHN, in Errol, 1782. [NAS.E326.1.102]

SPENCE, DAVID, [1704-1766]. [Kilspindie MI]

SPRUNT, DAVID, mason in Errol, wife Mary Duff [1732-1762]. [Errol MI]

SPRUNT, JAMES, [1734-1824]. [Kinfauns MI]

STEEL, DAVID, [1753-1837], a farmer in Carmichaels, wife Helen Mitchell [1756-1833]. [Longforgan MI]

STEEL, ..., [1713-1792, died in Flawcraig, wife Elizabeth Clunnie [1716-1794]. [Kinnaird MI]

STEVENSON, Reverend ARCHIBALD, in St Madoes, 1782. [NAS.E326.1.102]

STEWART, ALLAN, [1736-1787], minister at Kilspindie 1762-1787, wife Helen Robertson [1745-1814], parents of Margaret, Alexander, Robert, Alexander, Archibald, Allan, Helen, and William. [Kilspindie MI][NAS.E326.1.102][F.IV.215]

STEWART, JOHN, schoolmaster at Kinfauns, 1725. [NAS.CH1.2.50.fos.200-206]

STEWART, Lt. Gen. ROBERT, of Rait, [1745-1820]. [Kilspindie MI]

STIVEN, JAMES, a hammerman in Errol, 1682. [HL#1091]

STODDART, DAVID, in Kinfauns, 1782. [NAS.E326.1.102]

STOUT, ALEXANDER, an indweller in Errol, 1681/1682. [HL#1084/1091]

SWAN, MARGARET, relict of John Monro tenant of 'Midwifesrowm' in the parish of Errol, 1728. [HL#77]

SWINTON, PATRICK, formerly a boatman in Errol, 1739. [NAS.CH2.887.7]

SYMMER, GEORGE, minister at Kilspindie from 1615 to 1622. [F.4.214]

TAYLOR, GEORGE, in Errol, 1662. [RGS.XI.265]

TAYLOR, GEORGE, born 1669, married, in Leyes, 1709. [HL#64]

TAYLOR, JOHN, born 1681, married, in Leyes, 1709. [HL#64]

TAYLOR, KATHERINE, in Errol, 1739. [NAS.CH2.887.7]

TAYLOR, MATHEW, in Kilspindie, 1673. [HL#21]

TAYLOR, PETER, born 1670, unmarried, in Leyes, 1709. [HL#64]

TAYLOR, PETER, [1758-1828], a tailor on Chapelhill, husband of Isobel Donald [1755-1829]. [St Madoes MI]

THOMSON, DAVID, church seat rent, Inchture, 1772-1773. [NAS.CH2.188.1.291]

THOMSON, GEORGE, an old man, once a merchant in Errol, 1739. [NAS.CH2.887.7]

THOMSON, ISABEL, a widow with two children in Errol, 1739. [NAS.CH2.887.7]

TILLOCH, ANDREW, an old tailor in Errol, 1739. [NAS.CH2.887.7]

TODD, WILLIAM, [1756-1815], wife Isabel Inglis, [1764-1844]. [St Madoes MI]

TURNBULL, GEORGE, church seat rent, Inchture, 1771-1773. [NAS.CH2.188.1.291]

TURNBULL, THOMAS, of Bogmilne, 1718. [HL#73]

TYLER, JAMES, indweller in Flawcraig, wife Elspeth Foord [1650-1691]. [Rait MI]

WALES, JAMES, servant to Gilbert Jackson, 1671. [HL#10]

WALLACE, PATRICK, schoolmaster at Errol, 1695, 1709. [HL#64/1124]]

WATSON, ALEXANDER, and his wife Barbara Monorgan, in Kingoodie, Longforgan, 1665. [RGS.X.813]

WATSON, ALEXANDER, in Errol, 1677. [HL#1070]

WATSON, THOMAS, tenant farmer in Longly, husband of Elspeth Imrie [1752-1777], parents of Thomas [1777-1778]. [Kinfauns MI]

WEDDERSPOON, JAMES, [1744-1817], wood-keeper in Balthayock, husband of Janet Speedie. [Kinfauns MI]

WEDDERBURN, Sir JOHN, in Inchture, 1782. [NAS.E326.1.102]

WEMYSS, THOMAS, in Longforgan, 1782. [NAS.E326.1.102]

WHITE, EUPHAN, in Errol, 1744. [NAS.CH2.877.7.66]

WHITEHEAD, THOMAS, a tenant in South Leyes, 1709. [HL#64]

WHITEHEAD, WILLIAM, son of Patrick Whitehead in Pitrodie, 1691. [HL#68]

WILKIE, ANDREW, in the East end of Errol, 1662. [RGS.XI.264]

WILL, ALEXANDER, [1693-1774], a saddler in Pitmiddie. [Kinnaird MI]

WILLIAMSON, DAVID, minister at Kilspindie 1600-1605, 1622-1646, died 1646, husband of (1) Bessie Wedderburn, (2) Margaret Johnston, father of David, Margaret, Helen, and Agnes. [Kilspindie MI][F.IV.214]

WILSON, GEORGE, in Errol, 1662. [RGS.XI.265]

WILSON, THOMAS, died 1790, husband of Janet Duncan, died 1782, parents of Thomas Wilson a boat-wright in Inchyra. [St Madoes MI]

WRIGHT, Mrs, in Kilspindie, 1782. [NAS.E326.1.102]

YEAMAN, JAMES, in Errol, 1782. [NAS.E326.1.102]

YOUNG, ROBERT, [1734-1811], wife Ann Wanless [1727-1787]. [Longforgan MI]

REFERENCES and ABBREVIATIONS

Comm.	Commissariat
F	Fasti Ecclesiae Scoticanae
HL	Hay of Leys ms, University of St Andrews
MI	Monumental Inscription
NA	National Archives, London
NAS	National Archives of Scotland, Edinburgh
P	Prisoners of the '45
RGS	Register of the Great Seal of Scotland

ADIE, ELIZABETH, and her spouse William Johnstone, in Blackford, testament, 1677, Comm. Dunblane. [NAS]

AIRTH, ELSPETH, spouse to Alexander Willison in Kirkton of Auchterarder, testament, 1668, Comm. Dunblane. [NAS]

AITKEN, MARION, spouse to George Taylor, in Hill of Pitcellanie, Muthill, testament, 1662, Dunblane. [NAS]

ALEXANDER, ALEXANDER, in Pitkellonie, Muthill, testament, 1672, Comm. Dunblane. [NAS]

ALISE, JAMES, in Monk's Croft, Tullibardine, one of the Duke of Atholl's Fencible Men, 1706. [CAT.II]

ALICE, JOHN, at the Waulkmill of Fossaway, Auchterarder, testament, 1750, Comm. Dunblane. [NAS]

ALICE, ROBERT, of Blairingone, Auchterarder, deceased, and his daughters Janet, Susanna, Margaret, Euphame, Joan, and Christian, a deed, 1688. [NAS.GD160.23.7]

ALICE, ROBERT, in Auchterarder, 1762. [NAS.E326.1.99]

ALLAN, ANDREW, in Cowgask, Trinity Gask, testament, 1683, Comm. Dunblane. [NAS]

ALLAN, JAMES, born 1758, died 1810. [Crieff MI]

ALLAN, THOMAS, born 1756, died 1816.[Crieff MI]

ANDERSON, JOHN, in Kirkton, Tullibardine, one of the Duke of Atholl's Fencible Men, 1706. [CAT.II]

ANDERSON, THOMAS, 'preses' of the constables and elders of Forgandenny, a report, 1779. [NAS.B59.31.72]

ANDERSON, WILLIAM, in Ardach, Muthill, 1762. [NAS.E326.1.99]

ANGUS, ANDREW, and his spouse Marion Graham, in the Moor of Duncrub, Dunning, testament, 1664, Comm. Dunblane. [NAS]

ANNAND, JAMES, in Dunning, testament, 1781, Comm. Dunblane. [NAS]

ARCHER, ROBERT, in the Waulkmill of Ogilvy, Blackford, testament, 1672, Comm. Dunblane. [NAS]

ARMSTRONG, ROBERT, in Balloch, Muthill, testament, 1670, Comm. Dunblane. [NAS]

ARNOT, JAMES, born 1742, died 1793. [Fowlis Wester MI]

ARNOT, PETER, a merchant, died 1790, his wife Mary Miller, died 1790, their daughters Margaret and Ann died 1782, daughter Janet died 1802, son William died 1803. [Crieff MI]

ARNOT, SAMUEL, born 1731, tenant of the Hill of Ruhven, died 1787. [Crieff MI]

BAIN, ANDREW, a Roman Catholic in Boreland, Auchterarder, 1703. [NAS.CH1.2.5.2]

BAIN, MARGARET, relict of James Anderson in Braco, Muthill, testament, 1751, Comm. Dunblane. [NAS]

BAIRD, JOHN, minister at Dunning, 1797. [NAS.E326.10]

BALCANQUELL, WILLIAM, in Duthiestoun, Dunblane, testament, 1731, Comm. Dunblane. [NAS]

BALFOUR, JAMES, in Middlebowes, Dunblane, testament, 1685, Comm. Dunblane. [NAS]

BALLANTINE, JOHN, a farmer in Muckart, 1782. [NAS.E326.1.102]

BALMAIN, JAMES, born 1727, proprietor of Coull, died 1797. [Forteviot MI]

BALMAIN, JOHN, a shoemaker in Dunning, 1787. [NAS.B59.31.92]

BALMANNO, JOHN, in Aberdalgie, 1785. [NAS.E326.9.2]

BARCLAY, JAMES, born 1750, a smith at Castleton, died 1831, son of William Barclay born 1717, died 1769, and his wife Janet Hog, born 1719, died 1771, 33also his wife Helen Ritchie, born 1739, died 1805. [Fowlis Wester MI]

BAXTER, DAVID, a weaver in Murray of Niviland's factory, Crieff, a Jacobite in the Duke of Perth's Regiment in 1745, a rebel transported from Tilbury to the West Indies in 1747. [P.2.30]

BAYNE, JOHN, born 1688, a sievewright, died 1753, husband of Marjory Reid, born 1693, died 1746. [Forteviot MI]

BAYNE, JOHN, in Blackford, 1762. [NAS.E326.1.99]

BAYNE, PATRICK, of Findall, tacks of the teinds of the lands of Findall and Dargill, 1683. [NAS.GD160.199]

BEUGO, JOHN, born 1744, minister at Dunning, died 1805, husband of Euphemia Baird, died 1786. [Dunning MI]

BLACK, DONALD, in Braco, Muthill, testament, 1606, Comm. Dunblane. [NAS]

BLACK, JOHN, sometime servitor to George Drummond of Callendar, testament, 1699, Comm. Dunblane. [NAS]

BLAIR, ALEXANDER, tenant in Findonie, Dunning, a charter, 1653. [NAS.GD56.74]

BLAIR, ALEXANDER, of Corbes, Dunning, testament, 1656, Comm. Dunblane. [NAS]

BLAYD, ALEXANDER, born 1696, died 1735. [Aberdalgie MI]

BLAYD, WILLIAM, born 1663, died 1699. [Aberdalgie MI]

BOOT, JAMES, in Gleneagles, Blackford, testament, 1667, Comm. Dunblane. [NAS]

BRANDER, AGNES, born 1713 in Kinloss, Moray, died 1787 in Crieff. [Crieff MI]

BRANDER, ANDREW, born 1754, died 1827, wife Betty McAllihatton, born 1737, died 1813. [Crieff MI]

BRANZEAN, WILLIAM, in Blacksauch, Blackford, testament, 1686, Comm. Dunblane. [NAS]

BRIDIE, JOHN, in Muthill, 1762. [NAS.E326.1.99]

BRIDIE, Mrs, in Muthill, 1762. [NAS.E326.1.99]

BROUGH, EDWARD, born 1741, a wright in Crieff, died 1797, his wife Isabella born 1740, died 1802. [Crieff MI]

BROUGH, Mrs, in East Miln, Auchterarder, 1762. [NAS.E326.1.99]

BROWN, ELISABETH, born 1716, died 1778, wife of David Porteous an innkeeper in Crieff. [Crieff MI]

BROWN, GEORGE, born 1647, a wright and farmer, died 1710, husband of Isobel Mitchell, died 1730. [Forteviot MI]

BROWN, HENRY, in Drummond, Muthill, testament, 1676, Comm. Dunblane. [NAS]

BROWN, MARGARET, a Roman Catholic in Auchterarder, 1703. [NAS.CH1.2.5.2]

BRUCE, ROBERT, of Bordie, Commissary of Dunblane pre 1691. [NAS.CC6.15.7]

BRUCE, WILLIAM, a farmer in Muckart, 1782. [NAS.E326.1.102]

BRUGH, JAMES, of Fossilmiln, born 1694, died 1758, husband of Janet Foot, born 1691, died 1764. [Auchterder, Main Street MI]

BRYCE, DAVID, in Calziechat, Kilmadock, testament, 1606, Comm. Dunblane. [NAS]

BRYCE, JAMES, in Milntown, Tullibardine, one of the Duke of Atholl's Fencible Men, 1706. [CAT.II]

BRYDIE, JOHN, a maltman in Muthill, testament, 1775, Comm. Dunblane. [NAS]

BUCHAN, JOHN, in Castleton, Fowlis Wester, testament, 1759, Comm. Dunblane. [NAS]

BUCHANAN, DUGALD, the Gaelic poet, schoolmaster and catechist at Glenartney, 1742. [NAS.CH1.2.84.89]

BUCHANAN, JOHN, born 1724, from Auchterarder, a Jacobite, transported from Liverpool aboard the _Gildart_ bound for Virginia on 24

February 1747, landed at Port North Potomac, Maryland, on 5 August 1747. [TNA.T1.328][P.2.60]

BULL, MARGARET, in Dunning, testament, 1781, Comm. Dunblane. [NAS]

BUNKILL, THOMAS, in Tullibardine, testament, 1622, Comm. Dunblane. [NAS]

BURDOUN, JAMES, eldest son of Harry Burdoun, a sasine of land in the parish of Muthill, 1659. [NAS.GD1.406.9]

BURDOUN, JOHN, and his spouse Katherine McLaren, in Auchingarrich, 3Muthill, testament, 1687, Comm. Dunblane. [NAS]

BURGH, WILLIAM, in Auchterarder, testament, 1780, Comm. Dunblane. [NAS]

BURT, JOHN, a tenant in Thanesland, Dunning, a sasine, 1737. [NAS.GD56.111]

CAIRNS, JOHN, in Carrin, Blackford, testament, 1687, Comm. Dunblane. [NAS]

CAMPBELL, ISOBEL, eldest daughter of Duncan Campbell, tenant in the Mains of Gorthie, Fowlis, and his wife Mary Fisken, testament, 1778, Comm. Dunblane. [NAS]

CAMPBELL, or MCGREGOR, JAMES, from Crieff, a piper in Glengyle's Regiment, a Jacobite transported from Liverpool aboard the Elizabeth bound for Jamaica on 6 February 1748, landed on Antigua on 21 March 1748. [TNA.T53.44][P.2.94]

CAMPBELL, JAMES, in Crieff, a deed of factory, 1774. [NAS.RD2.220.1523]

CANONOCH, DUNCAN, in Feddal, Muthill, testament, 1721, Comm. Dunblane. [NAS]

CARDNY, PATRICK, of Clachladrum, Fowlis, testament, 1618, Comm. Dunblane. [NAS]

CARMICHAEL, WILLIAM, a tailor in Abernethy, testament, 1612, Comm. Dunblane. [NAS]

CAW, JAMES, born 1714, died 1791, his wife Mary Gray, born 1721, died 1791, children Thomas, born 1753, died 1776, Alexander, born 1759, Christian, John and David all died as infants, James, born 1751, died 1820, and William. [Crieff MI]

CAW, JEAN, in Dunning, testament, 1781, Comm. Dunblane. [NAS]

CAW, LUDOVICK, a surgeon from Crieff, a Jacobite and surgeon in the Duke of Perth's Regiment in 1745. [SHS.8.42]

CAW, THOMAS, son of the late Thomas Caw in Crieff, a bond, 1716. [NAS.GD1.1288.35]

CHALMERS, ALEXANDER, of Inverdunning, Dunning, 1797. [NAS.E326.10]; his wife Margaret Bonar, born 1750, died 1796. [Dunning MI]

CHALMERS, GEORGE, in Thainsland, Dunning, testament, 1665, Comm. Dunblane. [NAS]

CHAPMAN, JOHN, tenant in Findonie, Dunning, a charter, 1653; testament, 1670, Comm. Dunblane. [NAS. GD56.74]

CHAPMAN, MARGARET, and her spouse Robert Malice, in Abernethy, testament, 1669, Comm. Dunblane. [NAS]

CHRISTIE, DAVID, a farmer in Nether Broadslap, Dunning, 1797. [NAS.E326.10]

CHRISTIE, WILLIAM, in Dunning, testament, 1684, Comm. Dunblane. [NAS]

CLARK, ARCHIBALD, a piper in Abernethy, and his spouse Emily Williamson, testament, 1663, Comm. Dunblane. [NAS]

CLARK, JOHN, born 1739, a farmer in Keillour, died 1820, husband of Mary Anderson, born 1749, died 1823. [Fowlis Wester MI]

CLEMENT, JAMES, a tenant in Kintocher, Fowlis, testament, 1752, Comm. Dunblane. [NAS]

CLOVE, JOHN, in Monk's Croft, Tullibardine, one of the Duke of Atholl's Fencible Men, 1706. [CAT.II]

CLOW, ANDREW, born 1739, a farmer in Crieff Vechtor, died 1805, husband of Catherine Stiven. [Crieff MI]

CLOW, DAVID, in Douchly, Blackford, 1762. [NAS.E326.1.99]; testament, 1781, Comm. Dunblane. [NAS]

CLUNY, DAVID, in Abernethy, testament, 1757, Comm. Dunblane. [NAS]

COCHRANE, GEORGE, in Cumblieburn, Blackford, testament, 1687, Comm. Dunblane. [NAS]

COCK, JAMES, in Clathick, Comrie, testament, 1685, Comm. Dunblane. [NAS]

COKE, JOHN, in Delanross, Comrie, testament, 1667, Comm. Dunblane. [NAS]

COLDSTREAM, ALEXANDER, in Muthill, 1762. [NAS.E326.1.99; GD1.392.213]

COLDSTREAM, JOHN, born 1676, a schoolmaster, died 1746, husband of Elizabeth Reid. [Fowlis Wester MI]; testament, 1750, Comm. Dunblane. [NAS]

COLT, THOMAS, of Busbie, Methven, testament, 1656, Comm. Dunblane. [NAS]

COMRIE, ALEXANDER, born 1740, died 1805. [Comrie MI]

COMRIE, DUNCAN, from Woodend of Mevie, Comrie, a Jacobite in 1745. [SHS.8.44]

COMRIE, PATRICK, in Laggan, Comrie, testament, 1774, Comm. Dunblane. [NAS]

CONDIE, THOMAS, in Balwhandie, Dunning, testament, 1671, Comm. Dunblane. [NAS]

COOK, JOHN, in Crieff, 1785. [NAS.E326.9.2]

CRAIGIE, MARGARET, spouse of Robert Imbrie in Abernethy, testament, 1618, Comm. Dunblane. [NAS]

CRAMB, JAMES, a merchant in Buttergask, testament, 1751, Comm. Dunblane. [NAS]

CRAMBIE, ROBERT, in Dunning, testament, 1632, Comm. Dunblane. [NAS]

CRAWFORD, ALEXANDER, a gardener at Machany, Blackford, testament, 1748, Comm. Dunblane. [NAS]

CRAWFORD, ROBERT, a tenant in Thanesland, Dunning, a sasine, 1737. [NAS.GD56.111]

CRICHTOUN, MARGARET, spouse to George Brown of Meiklebuttergask, testament, 1659, Comm. Dunblane. [NAS]

CRUICKSHANK, ALEXANDER, in Muthill, 1786. [NAS.CH12.24.620]

CUNNINGHAM, WILLIAM, son of the late William Cunningham, a tailor in Abernethy, testament, 1711, Comm. Dunblane. [NAS]

CUTHBERT, THOMAS, in Over Gask, testament, 1677, Comm. Dunblane. [NAS]

DAES, JOHN, in Forteviot, letters, 1728. [NAS.B59.38.2.49]

DARLING, JOHN, a cordiner at the Milton of Auchterarder, testament, 1621, Comm. Dunblane. [NAS]

DAVIDSON, JAMES, a vintner in Muthill, deeds, 1780-1795. [NAS.GD160.493]

DAVIDSON, JOHN, in Ogilvie Miln, Blackford, 1762. [NAS.E326.1.99]

DAVIDSON, WILLIAM, in Auchterarder, testament, 1781, Comm. Dunblane. [NAS]

DAVIDSON, Mrs, in Auchterarder, 1762. [NAS.E326.1.99]

DAWSON, WILLIAM, in Culquhattock, Muthill, testament, 1599, Comm. Dunblane. [NAS]

DEAN, BESSIE, spouse to William Barclat in Pitcarlie, Abernethy, testament, 1617, Comm. Dunblane. [NAS]

DEAS, DAVID, born 1717, youngest son of Laurence Deas of East Mains of Aberdalgie, died 1741. [Aberdalgie MI]

DEAS, NICOL, tenant in Cree of Invermay, husband of Ann Williamson born 1730, died 1786. [Forteviot MI]

DEMPSTER, LAURENCE, schoolmaster of Forgandenny, accounts, 1758-1786. [NAS.GD347.62]

DEWAR, ANNA, a Roman Catholic in Auchterarder, 1703. [NAS.CH1.2.5.2]

DEWAR, JOHN, born 1748, died 1805. [Fowlis Webster MI]

DEWAR, MARGARET, in Dalhurley, Muthill, testament, 1735, Comm. Dunblane. [NAS]

DOCHERDICK, DONALD, in Port, Comrie, testament, 1665, Comm. Dunblane. [NAS]

DONALDSON, DAVID, a farmer in Upper Broadslap, Dunning, 1797. [NAS.E326.10]

DONALDSON, JAMES, a weaver in Dunning, testament, 1781, Comm. Dunblane. [NAS]

DONALDSON, JOHN, a burgess of Auchterarder, a sasine, 1655. [NAS.GD160.23.2]

DONALDSON, JOHN, in Rhynd, 1785. [NAS.E326.9.2]

DONALDSON, LAWRENCE, born 1684, died 1730, husband of Jean Rintoul. [Forteviot MI]

DONALDSON, WILLIAM, in Whitehills, Tullibardine, one of the Duke of Atholl's Fencible Men, 1706. [CAT.II]

DOUGALL, ARCHIBALD, the elder. A miller at Ballowmiln, Abernethy, testament, 1705, Comm. Dunblane. [NAS]

DOUGALL, ROBERT, in Auchterarder, testament, 1781, Comm. Dunblane. [NAS]

DOUGLAS, GEORGE, a cooper at Caldstream of Keir, testament, 1736, Comm. Dunblane. [NAS]

DOUGLAS, MARY, relict of John Baxter a shoemaker in Auchterarder, testament, 1765, Comm. Dunblane. [NAS]

DOW, JAMES, in Glenlichorn, Muthill, testament, 1748, Comm. Dunblane. [NAS]

DOW, PETER, born 1728, a merchant, died in Glasgow in 1784, buried at Fowlis Wester, father of James Dow a merchant in Crieff. [Fowlis Wester MI]

DRON, JEAN, in Clow, Dunning, testament, 1666, Comm. Dunblane. [NAS]

DRON, WILLIAM, a farmer in the Mains of Aberdalgie, 1797. [NAS.E326.10]

DRUMMOND, ADAM, in Muthill, 1762. [NAS.E326.1.99]

DRUMMOND, ALEXANDER, a Roman Catholic priest in Auchterarder, 1714. [NLS.ms976/143]

DRUMMOND, ANDREW, of Drummaquhance, Muthill, testament, 1756, Comm. Dunblane. [NAS]

DRUMMOND, COLIN, in Monk's Croft, Tullibardine, one of the Duke of Atholl's Fencible Men, 1706. [CAT.II]

DRUMMOND, DAVID, in Muthill, 1762. [NAS.E326.1.99]

DRUMMOND, EDWARD, a Roman Catholic in Auchterarder, 1703. [NAS.CH1.2.5.2]

DRUMMOND, ELIZABETH, born 1751, died 1821, spouse of John Robertson a tenant in Gorthy Mains. [Fowlis Wester MI]

DRUMMOND, GAVIN, a brewer from Auchterarder, a Jacobite in 1745. [SHS.8.44]

DRUMMOND, JAMES, of Breich, testament, 1664, Comm. Dunblane. [NAS]

DRUMMOND, Dr JAMES, minister at Muthill, letters, 1680-1683. [NAS.B59.25.1.20; B59.28.41]

DRUMMOND, JAMES, a Roman Catholic in Auchterarder, 1703. [NAS.CH1.2.5.2]

DRUMMOND, JAMES, schoolmaster at Glenroar, 1744. [NAS.CH1.2.84.fo.63]

DRUMMOND, JAMES, a smith in Auchterarder, testament, 1758, Comm. Dunblane. [NAS]

DRUMMOND, JAMES, in Muthill, 1762. [NAS.E326.1.99]

DRUMMOND, JANET, relict of Thomas Mailer a burgess of Auchterarder, a wadset, 1657. [NAS.GD220.1C.2.3.2]

DRUMMOND, JOHN, son and heir of George Drummond of Balloch, 1656. [RGS.X.661]

DRUMMOND, JOHN, a merchant in Muthill, husband of Elspeth Ferguson, deeds, 1660s. [NAS.GD155.58]

DRUMMOND, JOHN, the elder of Pitkellenie, a Roman Catholic in Auchterarder, 1703. [NAS.CH1.2.5.2]

DRUMMOND, JOHN, of Fairnton, and Marjory Gray, a marriage contract, 1707. [NAS.GD160.239]

DRUMMOND, JOHN, the stampmaster of Auchterarder, testament, 1745, Comm. Dunblane. [NAS]

DRUMMOND, JOHN, of Culcrief, born 1688, died 1772. [Crieff MI]

DRUMMOND, JOHN, a farmer in Dunning, 1782; 1785. [NAS.E326.1.102; 9.2]

DRUMMOND, JOHN, of Keltie, born 1733, died 1801. [Dunning MI]

DRUMMOND, LEWIS, a Roman Catholic in Auchterarder, 1703. [NAS.CH1.2.5.2]

DRUMMOND, LUDOVICK, of Wester Feddals, a Roman Catholic in Auchterarder, 1703. [NAS.CH1.2.5.2]

DRUMMOND, Mrs MARY, in Thornhill, Muthill, 1762. [NAS.E326.1.99]

DRUMMOND, ROBERT, minister at Auchterarder, 1762. [NAS.E326.1.99]

DRUMMOND, ROBERT, in Muthill, 1785. [NAS.E326.9.2]

DRUMMOND, THOMAS, in Innerpeffrey, and his spouse Helen Drummond, were granted Kirkhill, Auchterarder, in 1624. [NAS.GD160.19.20]

DRUMMOND, THOMAS, in Auchterarder, 1762. [NAS.E326.1.99]

DRYSDALE, JAMES, in Balwhandie, Dunning, testament, 1666, Comm. Dunblane. [NAS]

DRYSDALE, JOHN, born 1739, a farmer at Carsehead, died 1814, husband of Janet Ramsay, born 1739, died 1812. [Fowlis Wester MI]

DUFF, CHRISTIAN, in Dulator, Fowlis, testament, 1667, Comm. Dunblane. [NAS]

DUNCAN, ANDREW, in Farmtounof Machany, Blackford, testament, 1748, Comm. Dunblane. [NAS]

DUNCAN, JAMES, at Drumend of Gask, testament, 1748, Comm. Dunblane. [NAS]

DUNCAN, MALCOLM, in Milntown, Tullibardine, one of the Duke of Atholl's Fencible Men, 1706. [CAT.II]

DUNCAN, ROBERT, a brewer in Dunning, testament, 1757, Comm. Dunblane. [NAS]

DUNN, JAMES, born 1761, died 1794, husband of Elizabeth Morrison who died in 1834. [Kirkton of Auchterarder MI]

DUNN, JOHN, a brewer in Auchterarder, testament, 1745, Comm. Dunblane. [NAS]

DUNNING, KATHERINE, and her spouse James Bayne, in Dunning, testament, 1683, Comm. Dunblane. [NAS]

EADIE, ALEXANDER, tenant in Rashiehill, Dunning, testament, 1734, Comm. Dunblane. [NAS]

EDIE, JAMES, the elder, in Easthill, Tullibardine, one of the Duke of Atholl's Fencible Men, 1706. [CAT.II]

EDIE, JAMES, the younger, in Easthill, Tullibardine, one of the Duke of Atholl's Fencible Men, 1706. [CAT.II]

EDDIE, JAMES, born 1764, died at Oil Mill in 1809, husband of Jane Scott, born 1764, died 1811. [Auchterarder MI]

EDIE, ROBERT, in East Third, Tullibardine, one of the Duke of Atholl's Fencible Men, 1706. [CAT.II]

EDMISTON, JOHN, in Kirkton of Auchterarder, a letter of horning, 1629. [NAS.GD160.19.25]

EDMONSTONE, alias COWHIRD, JOHN, a smith in Abernethy, testament, 1622, Comm. Dunblane. [NAS]

EDMONSTONE, ROBERT, in Balgour, Dunning, testament, 1665, Comm. Dunblane. [NAS]

EISDALE, JAMES, in Drum of Garvock, Dunning, testament, 1662, Comm. Dunblane. [NAS]

ELDER, JAMES, at the Milton of Auchterarder, and his wife Nichola Whytburn, a contract, 1626. [NAS.GD160.19.22]; testament, 1658, Comm. Dunblane. [NAS]

ELDER, JOHN, of Balbuchie, 1623. [NAS.GD190.1.5]

ELISON, JAMES, in Brownhill, Innermay, Forteviot, testament, 1654, Comm. Dunblane. [NAS]

ERINOCH, JAMES, in Chalmerstrathie, Auchterarder, testament, 1688, Comm. Dunblane. [NAS]

ERSKINE, WILLIAM, a minister in Muthill, 1762. [NAS.E326.1.99]

EWAN, JAMES, born 1730, tenant of the Mill of Findinny, died 1787, husband of Betty Lawson, born 1742, died 1802. [Dunning MI]

EWAN, ROBERT, and his son John Ewan, in Auchterarder, 1635. [NAS.GD155.485]

EWING, ELSPETH, spouse to Robert Lourie in Abernethy, testament, 1662, Comm. Dunblane. [NAS]

FAICHNEY, BETHIA, in Muthill, 1762. [NAS.E326.1.99]

FAICHNEY, MARJORIE, in Allans, Muthill, testament, 1727, Comm. Dunblane. [NAS]

FALVIE, DAVID, in Laverock Land, Tullibardine, one of the Duke of Atholl's Fencible Men, 1706. [CAT.II]

FARG, JANET, a widow in Aberargie, testament, 1629, Comm. Dunblane. [NAS]

FARQUHAR, HENRY, a brewer in Aberargie, testament, 1653, Comm. Dunblane. [NAS]

FENTON, JAMES, of Milnearn, Trinity Gask, testament, 1753, Comm. Dunblane. +[NAS]

FERGUSON, WILLIAM, from Moevie, Comrie, a Jacobite in the Duke of Perth's Regiment, 1745, a prisoner in 1746. [P.2.190]

FERNIE, JOHN, in Wester Colsie, Abernethy, testament, 1616, Comm. Dunblane. [NAS]

FERRIER, JOHN, in Loaning, Tullibardine, one of the Duke of Atholl's Fencible Men, 1706. [CAT.II]

FINGASK, ARTHUR, in Meikle Cairn, Forteviot, testament, 1614, Comm. Dunblane. [NAS]

FINLAY, ROBERT, in Middle Faddles, Muthill, testament, 1734, Comm. Dunblane. [NAS]

FINNIE, JOHN, in Drumlochie, Blackford, testament, 1676, Comm. Dunblane. [NAS]

FISHER, JAMES, a farmer in Broom, Dunning, 1782, 1797. [NAS.E326.1.102; E326.10]

FISKEN, NINIAN, in Auchterarder, testament, 1778, Comm. Dunblane. [NAS]

FLEMING, MARGARET, spouse to the late Thomas Archer a weaver in Ardoch, Muthill, testament, 1793, Comm. Dunblane. [NAS]

FLOCKHART, NINIAN, a maltman in Dunning, 1687.[NAS.GD56.92]

FOOT, ROBERT, in Auchterarder, testament, 1743, Comm. Dunblane. [NAS]

FORBES, DANIEL, at the Bridge of Ardoch, Muthill, a petition, 1788. [NAS.B59.31.101]

FORBES, WILLIAM, a surgeon in Muthill, testaments, 1771/1781, Comm. Dunblane. [NAS]

FORFAR, BEATRIX, wife of John Smith in Abernethy, testament, 1615, Comm. Dunblane. [NAS]

FOTHRINGHAM, JANET, late spouse to William Arnot in Gascovie, Abernethy, testament, 1611, Comm. Dunblane. [NAS]

FRANCE, JAMES, in Blackford, testament, 1672, Comm. Dunblane. [NAS]

FRANCE, JAMES, in Park, Tullibardine, one of the Duke of Atholl's Fencible Men, 1706. [CAT.II]

FRANCE, NEIL, in Wester Newton, Tullibardine, one of the Duke of Atholl's Fencible Men, 1706. [CAT.II]

FRANCE, WILLIAM, the elder, in West Park Tullibardine, one of the Duke of Atholl's Fencible Men, 1706. [CAT.II]

FRANCE, WILLIAM, the younger, in West Park Tullibardine, one of the Duke of Atholl's Fencible Men, 1706. [CAT.II]

FRASER, DONALD, a flaxdresser in Crieff, died 1772, his wife Margaret Taylor died 1787. [Crieff MI]

FRASER, WILLIAM, in Easter Keillour, Fowlis, testament, 1687, Comm. Dunblane. [NAS]

FRAZER, WILLIAM, born 1683, died 1748, husband of Christian Simpson, born 1693, died 1756. [Dunning MI]

FRASER, WILLIAM, a farmer in Bogtown Ley, Forteviot, 1797. [NAS.E326.10]

FREEBAIRN, ROBERT, in Wester Lumbenie, Abernethy, testament, 1688, Comm. Dunblane. [NAS]

FREELAND, JANET, relict of Richard Dae, in East Mains of Aberdalgie, testament, 1657, Comm. Dunblane. [NAS]

FRENCH, ROBERT, and his spouse Janet More, in Smiddiehaugh of Aberruthven, a wadset, 1656. [NAS.GD220.1.C.2.6.1]

FRISKEN, WILLIAM, in Dupplin, testament, 1673, Comm. Dunblane. [NAS]

FULTON, WILLIAM, born 1692, died 1767, husband of Janet Dobson, born 1694, died 1767. [Auchterarder, Aberruthven MI]

FYFE, JAMES, of Dron, a sasin witness, 1717.[NAS.GD68.1.293]

FYFE, JOHN, a carrier in Abernethy, testament, 1662, Comm. Dunblane. [NAS]

GALL, DAVID, servant to Robert McKinnon in Dunning, testament, 1672, Comm. Dunblane. [NAS]

GARDNER, ANDREW, in West Mains, Tullibardine, one of the Duke of Atholl's Fencible Men, 1706. [CAT.II]

GARDNER, HELEN, born 1709, died 1758, wife of Daniel Don Gorrie in Condieloch. [Fowlis Wester MI]

GARDNER, JOHN, a burgess of Auchterarder, a wadset, 1697. [NAS.GD220.1.C.2.5.5]

GARDNER, JOHN, in Blair Skaith, Tullibardine, one of the Duke of Atholl's Fencible Men, 1706. [CAT.II]

GARNOCK, ANDREW, in Smithyhill, later in Auchterarder, testament, 1774, Comm. Dunblane. [NAS]

GEDDES, THOMAS, son of the late Andrew Geddes, sometime in Carpow, Abernethy, testament, 1679, Comm. Dunblane. [NAS]

GENTLE, JAMES, in Bucknie Hill, Tullibardine, one of the Duke of Atholl's Fencible Men, 1706. [CAT.II]

GENTLE, MATHEW, in Bowhouse of Machany, Trinity Gask, testament, 1754, Comm. Dunblane. [NAS]

GENTLE, THOMAS, in Laverock Land, Tullibardine, one of the Duke of Atholl's Fencible Men, 1706. [CAT.II]

GEORGE, JOHN, born 1715, tenant in Carspin, died 1772, husband of Katherine Mailer. [Kirkton of Auchterarder MI]

GERRIE, DONALD, in Condolick, Fowlis, testament, 1652, Comm. Dunblane. [NAS]

GIBB, WILLIAM, servant to John Strathie, in West Fordun, Auchterarder, testament, 1733, Comm. Dunblane. [NAS]

GIBSON, JEAN, died in 1673, wife of Robert Elder the younger in Milton of Auchterarder. [Kirkton of Auchterarder MI]

GIBSON, MARGARET, a Roman Catholic in Balloch, Auchterarder, 1703. [NAS.CH1.2.5.2]

GIBSON, SOPHIA, relict of William Duncan tenant of Wester Rossie, Auchterarder, testament, 1739, Comm. Dunblane. [NAS]

GIBSON, THOMAS, died 1739. [Kirkton of Auchterarder MI]

GILBERT, JOHN, servant to John Annat in Braehead of Dunning, testament, 1666, Comm. Dunblane. [NAS]

GILLIES, JAMES, in Louche Mill, Abernethy, testament, testament, 1629, Comm. Dunblane. [NAS]

GILLIM, JOHN, a weaver in Dunning, testament, 1683, Comm. Dunblane. [NAS]

GILMOIR, CHRISTIAN, spouse of William Paterson in Loanhead of Baigle, Dron, testament, 1663, Comm. Dunblane. [NAS]

GILMOIR, HARRY, in Drumlochie, Blackford, testament, 1685, Comm. Dunblane. [NAS]

GILMORE, JOHN, tack of the Kirklands of Dron, 1689. [NAS.CH2.299.59]

GIRVAN, JOHN, in Kirkton, Tullibardine, one of the Duke of Atholl's Fencible Men, 1706. [CAT.II]

GLASS, JAMES, in Crieff, 1785. [NAS.E326.9.2]

GLOAG, ANDREW, died 1648, husband of Euphan Swinton, died 1655. [Dunning MI]

GLOAG, HERCULES, son of the late William Gloag, in Drumsauchie, Muthill, testament, 1748, Comm. Dunblane. [NAS]

GLOAG, WILLIAM, a writer in Dunning, a sasine, 1740. [NAS.GD56.112]

GLOAG, WILLIAM, a farmer in Dunning, 1782. [NAS.E326.1.102]

GOODWILLY, MITCHELL, in Pitlour, Abernethy, testament, 1703, Comm. Dunblane. [NAS]

GORRIE, JOHN, in Condecleuch, Fowlis, testament, 1728, Comm. Dunblane. [NAS]

GOTHRAY, JOHN, in Innerdunning, testament, 1664, Comm. Dunblane. [NAS]

GOVERNOUR, JAMES, in Cruttack, Muthill, testament, 1783, Comm. Dunblane. [NAS]

GOW, JANET, relict of John McEwan, in Wester Couden, Muthill, testament, 1763, Comm. Dunblane. [NAS]

GOWANS, JAMES, a farmer in Pittentian, died 1795, husband of Mary Oswald. [Crieff MI]

GOWANS, JEAN, born 1735, daughter of William Gowans and his wife Janet Moray, died 1757. [Crieff MI]

GOWANS, THOMAS, a labourer, formerly in Dunning, later in Fife, and his wife Ann Smith, who married in 1789, process of divorce, 1797. [NAS.CS8.6.1011]

GRAHAM, DAVID, of Braco, Fowlis, a deed, 1715. [NAS.RD3.145.880]; testament, 1720, Comm. Dunblane. [NAS]

GRAHAM, DAVID, in Muthill, 1785. [NAS.E326.9.2]

GRAHAM, JAMES, of Garnock, a farmer in Dunning, 1797. [NAS.E326.10]

GRAHAM, JOHN, in Auchterarder, 1762. [NAS.E326.1.99]

GRAHAM, MUNGO, eldest son of David Graham of Gorthie, and his spouse Helen Murray, were granted the lands of Easter Over Gorthie, parish of Fowlis, on 17 June 1657. [RGS.X.598]

GRAHAM, PATRICK, an apothecary in Redford, Crieff, emigrated to Georgia by 1736. [TNA.CO5.670.284]

GRAHAM, PATRICK, in Crieff, 1785. [NAS.E326.9.2]

GRAHAM, ROBERT, a Jacobite from Gorthie, Fowlis, a Commissary in 1745. [shs.8.44]

GRAHAM, THOMAS, in Methven, 1785. [NAS.E326.9.2]

GRAHAM, WILLIAM, in Muthill, 1785. [NAS.E326.9.2]

GRAHAM, Mrs, in Orchall, Muthill, 1762. [NAS.E326.1.99]

GRAME, JAMES, a farmer in Dunning, 1782. [NAS.E326.1.102]

GRAME, ROBERT, a farmer in Dunning, 1782. [NAS.E326.1.102]

GRANAR, JOHN, born 1585, died 1645. [Kirkton of Auchterarder MI]

GRAY, JEAN, in Boreland of Drummond, Muthill, testament, 1715, Comm. Dunblane. [NAS]

GRAYSICH, JANET, in Dullator, Fowlis, testament, 1667, Comm. Dunblane. [NAS]

GREGOR, JOHN, in Easter Keillour, Fowlis, testament, 1685, Comm. Dunblane. [NAS]

GUILD, DONALD, in Damahillies, Blackford, testament, 1745, Comm. Dunblane. [NAS]

GUILD, PATRICK, in Milne, Tullibardine, one of the Duke of Atholl's Fencible Men, 1706. [CAT.II]

HALDANE, DAVID, of Aberruthven, a deed 1715. [NAS.RD4.116.639]; testament, 1736, Comm. Dunblane. [NAS]

HALDANE, GEORGE, of Gleneagles, Blackford, 1785, [NAS.E326.9.2]; testament, 1785, Comm. Dunblane. [NAS]

HALDANE, JOHN, in West Mains, Tullibardine, one of the Duke of Atholl's Fencible Men, 1706. [CAT.II]

HALDANE, ROBERT, in Blackford, 1762. [NAS.E326.1.99]

HALLY, GEORGE, in North Kingkell, Trinity Gask, testament, 1731, Comm. Dunblane. [NAS]

HALLEY, JAMES, in Middle Third, Tullibardine, one of the Duke of Atholl's Fencible Men, 1706. [CAT.II]

HALLY, MARGARET, relict of William Bell a mason in Auchterarder, testament, 1731, Comm. Dunblane. [NAS]

HALLEY, WILLIAM, in Middle Third, Tullibardine, one of the Duke of Atholl's Fencible Men, 1706. [CAT.II]

HALSON, THOMAS, in Burnfoot of Kingkell, Trinity Gask, testament, 1754, Comm. Dunblane. [NAS]

HAMPBELL, JOHN, a tailor on the Moor of Duncrub, Dunning, testament, 1675, Comm. Dunblane. [NAS]

HARDIE, JOHN, minister at Aberdalgie, testament, 1688, Comm. Dunblane. [NAS]

HARLEY, JOHN, a farmer in Broom, Dunning, 1797. [NAS.E326.10]

HARRELL, WILLIAM, from Strothell Mill, Muthill, a Jacobite soldier in 1745. [SHS.8.46]

HARROWER, JAMES, in Drakemyres, Muthill, testament, 1729, Comm. Dunblane. [NAS]

HAY, HUGH, in Arngask, 1785. [NAS.E326.9.2]

HAY, JOSEPH, a vintner in Aberdargie, Abernethy, testament, 1784, Comm. Dunblane. [NAS]

HENDERSON, GEORGE, a baillie of Abernethy, testament, 1782, Comm. Dunblane. [NAS]

HENDERSON, Colonel JOHN, in Auchterarder, 1785. [NAS.E326.9.2]

HENDERSON, JOHN, born 1733, tenant in Wester Balquhandy, died 1795. [Dunning MI]

HENDERSON, PETER, in Dalreoch, Auchterarder, 1762. [NAS.E326.1.99]

HENDERSON, WILLIAM, in Dunblane, testament, 1793, Comm. Dunblane. [NAS]

HENDRY, ANDREW, born 1706, a resident of the Mill of Buchanty, died 1742. [Fowlis Wester MI]

HENDRY, WILLIAM, and his spouse Janet Rutherford, in Easter Keillour, Fowlis, testament, 1744, Comm. Dunblane. [NAS]

HEPBURN, DAVID, in Bucknie Hill, Tullibardine, one of the Duke of Atholl's Fencible Men, 1706. [CAT.II]

HEPBURN, DAVID, in Tullibardine, Blackford, testament, 1737, Comm. Dunblane. [NAS]

HEPBURN, JOHN, a farmer in Forteviot, 1782; 1785. [NAS.E326.1.102; 9.2]

HEPBURN, THOMAS, in Trinity Gask, 1785. [NAS.E326.9.2]

HERDMAN, HARRY, in Kirkton, Tullibardine, one of the Duke of Atholl's Fencible Men, 1706. [CAT.II]

HERING, HELEN, spouse to John Sanders in Clow, Dunning, testament, 1621, Comm. Dunblane. [NAS]

HILTON, DAVID, and his spouse Janet Foot, at the Mill of Gleneagles, a contract, 1626. [NAS.GD160.19.22]

HILTON, THOMAS, a burgess of Auchterarder, and his heir David Hilton, a sasine, 1617. [NAS.GD160.19.10]

HOG, JAMES, and his spouse Christian Shoolbred, in Carpow, Abernethy, testament, 1685, Comm. Dunblane. [NAS]

HOGGAN, CATHERINE, spouse to John Chalmer in Dunning, testament, 1655, Comm. Dunblane. [NAS]

HOME, EDWARD, portioner of North Balquhandie, Dunning, testament, 1675, Comm. Dunblane. [NAS]

HOOD, WILLIAM, in Fargs Mill, Abernethy, testament, 1781, Comm. Dunblane. [NAS]

HORN, ANDREW, a shoemaker in Dunning, 1787. [NAS.B59.31.92]

HOUSTOUN, AGNES, in Over Ochley, Dunblane, testament, 1749, Comm. Dunblane. [NAS]

HOWIE, EMMA, relict of Hew Williamson in Carpow, testament, 1619, Comm. Dunblane. [NAS]

HUGO, MARGARET, a Roman Catholic inn Strageath, Auchterarder, 1703. [NAS.CH1.2.5.2]

HUMBILL, JOHN, a skinner in Dunblane, testament, 1605, Comm. Dunblane.

HUSTON, JAMES, born 1734, died 1814, husband of Mary Monteith, born 1725, died 1795, parents of Margaret and Mary. [Auchterarder, Main Street, MI]

HUTCHESON, ALLAN, in Abernethy, testament, 1615, Comm. Dunblane.

HUTSON, ALEXANDER, a tenant on the lands of Dalreoch and Balgour, parish of Dunning, 1695. [NAS.GD56.128]

HUTSON, ROBERT, in Dunning, testament, 1781, Comm. Dunblane.

HUTTON, JAMES, a weaver in Dunning, testament and inventory, 1671, Comm. Dunblane.

HUTTON, JOHN, in Upper Lawhill of Gask, Trinity Gask, testament, 1761, Comm. Dunblane.

ILSON, JOHN, in Garvock, Dunning, testament, 1680, Comm. Dunblane.

IMRIE, WILLIAM, in Fildie, Dron, testament, 1687, Comm. Dunblane.

INGLIS, HENRY, a minister at Forteviot, 1782; 1785. [NAS.E326.1.102; 9.2]

ISDAILL, JOHN, in Innerdunning, testament, 1669, Comm. Dunblane.

JACK, ALEXANDER, at the Mill of Feddals, Muthill, testament, 1742, Comm. Dunblane.

JACK, WILLIAM, in Silvertown, Muthill, testament, 1749, Comm. Dunblane.

JOHNMAN, WILLIAM, a farmer in Dalviach, Dunning, 1797. [NAS.E326.10]

JOHNSTONE, DOROTHY, and her spouse Patrick McAndrew, in Fowlis, testament, 1681, Comm. Dunblane.

JOHNSTON, or CLERK, JOHN, a burgess of Auchterarder, a deed, 1634. [NAS.GD160.21.3]

JOHNSTON, LAWRENCE, in West Dron, 1701. [NAS.GD305.1.153.75]

JOPP, BESSIE, and her spouse James Stirk in Abernethy, testament, 1666, Comm. Dunblane. [NAS]

KEIR, THOMAS, in Muthill, 1785. [NAS.E326.9.2]

KELTIE, ALEXANDER, a brewer in Dunning, testament, 1714, Comm. Dunblane. [NAS]

KELTIE, ROBERT, in Dunblane, 1762. [NAS.E326.1.99]

KEMPIE, PATRICK, in Drumfinn, Fowlis, testament, 1752, Comm. Dunblane. [NAS]

KEMPIE, PETER, born, overseer at Ochtertyre, died 1812. [Fowlis Wester MI]

KENNEDY, JOHN, gardener to Lord Drummond, a Roman Catholic in Auchterarder, 1703. [NAS.CH1.2.5.2]; testament 1746, Comm. Dunblane. [NAS]

KETTLE, ANDREW, a weaver in Fowlis, testament, 1750, Comm. Dunblane. [NAS]

KILGOUR, ROBERT, in Bin, Abernethy, testament, 1664, Comm. Dunblane. [NAS]

KILLOP, WILLIAM, a chapman in Dunning, testament, 1612, Comm. Dunblane. [NAS]

KINLOCH, AGNES, and her spouse James Noraway, in Cilzie, Abernethy, testament, 1670, Comm. Dunblane. [NAS]

KINMONTH, DAVID, born 1740, died 1800, husband of Mary Winton, born 1740, died 1815. [Dunning MI]

KIPPEN, THOMAS, in Dunning, testament, 1781, Comm. Dunblane. [NAS]

KYNOCH, DUNCAN, in West Park Tullibardine, one of the Duke of Atholl's Fencible Men, 1706. [CAT.II]

LAING, PATRICK, in Wester Coalsie, Abernethy, testament, 1742, Comm. Dunblane. [NAS]

LATHANGIE, HENRY, eldest son of Henry Lathangie of Ballingall, and his future wife Margaret Lathangie, daughter of Robert Lathangie a shoemaker in Forgandenny, a charter of one third of the lands of Ballingall, 1649. [NAS.GD29.694]

LAUDER, ALEXANDER, a farmer and cattle-dealer in Dron, 1798. [NAS.CS97.112.92]

LAURENCE, ANDREW, the younger, in Machany, testament, 1630, Comm. Dunblane. [NAS]

LAURENCE, ANDREW, in Milntown, Tullibardine, one of the Duke of Atholl's Fencible Men, 1706. [CAT.II]

LAUSON, Mrs, in Blackford, 1762. [NAS.E326.1.99]

LAW, THOMAS, and his wife Helen Walker, in Easter Keillour, Fowlis, testament, 1686, Comm. Dunblane. [NAS]

LAWSON, JOHN, in Milntown, Tullibardine, one of the Duke of Atholl's Fencible Men, 1706. [CAT.II]

LAWSON, WILLIAM, born 1765, a vintner in Auchterarder, died 1793, husband of Mary Graham. [Auchterarder, Main Street, MI]

LAWSON, WILLIAM, in Abernethy, sometime quartermaster on board the cutter Rattlesnake, testament, 1797, Comm. Dunblane. [NAS]

LEISHMAN, JOHN, in Drumfauld, Blackford, testament, 1668, Comm. Dunblane. [NAS]

LEITH, JOHN, in Greenock, Callendar, testament, 1673, Comm. Dunblane. [NAS]

LINDSAY, DAVID, a notary at Gorthie, Fowlis, testament, 1694, Comm. Dunblane. [NAS]

LITTLEJOHN, in West Mains, Tullibardine, one of the Duke of Atholl's Fencible Men, 1706. [CAT.II]

LITTLEJOHN, JOHN, a farmer in Auchterarder, 1797. [NAS.E326.10]

LITTLEJOHN, MARY, in Tullibardine, Blackford, testament, 1740, Comm. Dunblane. [NAS]

LOCKHART, JAMES, a wright in Crieff, a Jacobite in 1745. [SHS.8.46]

LOCHHEAD, WALTER, servant to Lord Rollo, in Dunning, testament, 1671, Comm. Dunblane. [NAS]

LORIMER BEATRICE, spouse to Patrick Wemyss in Abernethy, testament, 1611, Comm. Dunblane. [NAS]

LOUTFOOT, DAVID, in Monk's Croft, Tullibardine, one of the Duke of Atholl's Fencible Men, 1706. [CAT.II]

LOUTFOOT, JOHN, in Blair Skaith, Tullibardine, one of the Duke of Atholl's Fencible Men, 1706. [CAT.II]

LOUTFOOT, JOHN, in Wester Newton, Tullibardine, one of the Duke of Atholl's Fencible Men, 1706. [CAT.II]

LOUTFOOT, PATRICK, tenant in Parnie, Auchterarder, testament, 1753, Comm. Dunblane. [NAS]

LOW, JAMES, of Lednurquhart, Abernethy, testament, 1772, Comm. Dunblane. [NAS]

LOWRIE, GELIS, spouse to William Donald a smith in Aberdalgy, Abernethy, testament, 1616, Comm. Dunblane. [NAS]

LYELL, HEW, in Carpow, testament, 1629, Comm. Dunblane. [NAS]

MCALHONNELL, JAMES, in Glen Lichorn, Muthill, testament, 1741, Comm. Dunblane. [NAS]

MCANDREW, PATRICK, in Alichgrew, Muthill, testament, 1669, Comm. Dunblane. [NAS]

MCARA, DUNCAN, in Castleton, Fowlis, testament, 1686, Comm. Dunblane. [NAS]

MCCAIS, DAVID, in Aberargie, testament, 1668, Comm. Dunblane. [NAS]

MCCALL, ARCHIBALD, in Loaning, Tullibardine, one of the Duke of Atholl's Fencible Men, 1706. [CAT.II]

MCCALL, DAVID, born at Midshed of Gorthy in 1717, died at the Mains of Gorthy in 1782. [Fowlis Wester MI]

MCCLEISH, JOHN, minister at Gask, 1762. [NAS.E326.1.99]

MCCLEISH, WILLIAM, in Muthill, 1762. [NAS.E326.1.99]

MCCOMBIE, THOMAS, in Muthill, 1762. [NAS.E326.1.99]

MCCOMES, PETER, tenant in Ardoch, Fowlis Wester, testament, 1784, Comm. Dunblane. [NAS]

MCCOUNIE, DAVID, under-miller at Tullibardine Mill, testament, 1763, Comm. Dunblane. [NAS]

MCCULLOCH, JOHN, in Bridgehill, Muthill, testament, 1763, Comm. Dunblane. [NAS]

MCCURRICH, WILLIAM, born 1741, died at Loneside of Drummie, 1802, his wife Elizabeth Marshall, born 1743, died 1788. [Fowlis Wester MI]

MCDONALD, ALLAN, a brewer from Crieff, a Jacobite in 1745. [SHS. 8.46]

MCEWAN, WILLIAM, born 1766, a watchmaker in Auchterarder, died 1826, husband of Euphemia Imrie, born 1767, died 1851. [Auchterarder, Main Street, MI]

MCFARLAND, JAMES, born 1685, died 1745, father of John McFarland, born 1723, died 1747. [Crieff MI]

MCGIBBON, JAMES, born 1728, died 1802, husband of Jean Rogie, born 1750, died 1810. [Crieff MI]

MCGIBBON, MARGARET, a Roman Catholic in Balloch, Auchterarder, 1703. [NAS.CH1.2.5.2]

MCINNES, DONALD, in Wester Newton, Tullibardine, one of the Duke of Atholl's Fencible Men, 1706. [CAT.II]

MCINTOSH, LACHLAN, the chamberlain at Echo, a deed, 1703. [NAS.GD305.1.153.134]

MCINTYRE, DAVID, born 1769, a merchant in Crieff, died 1807. [Crieff MI]

MCLALEN, PETER, born 1724, died 1795, son of William McLalen and his wife Elizabeth Maxton, born 1723, died 1768. [Fowlis Wester MI]

MCLARIN, KATHERINE, born 1734, died 1803, wife of William Faichney a mason in Crieff. [Crieff MI]

MCLAUCHLANE, ELIZABETH, widow of George McFarlane a vintner in Crieff, a decreet, 1767. [NAS.CS16.1.130/49]

MCLAURIN, JOHN, born 1736, a farmer at Westburn of Strathy, died 1816, husband of Mary Gibbons. [Auchterarder, Aberruthven, MI]

MCLAWRIN, JAMES, born 1756, died 1806, husband of Ann Reoch, born 1744, died 1799. [Crieff MI]

MCLEAN, ANDREW, in East Third, Tullibardine, one of the Duke of Atholl's Fencible Men, 1706. [CAT.II]

MCLEAN, OWEN, a weaver from Tullochallan, Strathearn, a Jacobite who was transported to the colonies in 1747. [P.3.150]

MCLEISH, JOHN, in Loaning, Tullibardine, one of the Duke of Atholl's Fencible Men, 1706. [CAT.II]

MCLEISH, JOHN, a messenger in Muthill, 1715. [NAS.B59.30.3]

MCLEISH, JOHN, from Muthill, a Jacobite in 1745. [SHS.8.48]

MCLEISH, MALCOLM, a messenger in Muthill, husband of Janet White, parents of Jean McLeish, a bond, 1686. [NAS.GD155.401]

MCNAB, DUNCAN, in West Park Tullibardine, one of the Duke of Atholl's Fencible Men, 1706. [CAT.II]

MCNAB, PATRICK, in West Park Tullibardine, one of the Duke of Atholl's Fencible Men, 1706. [CAT.II]

MCNEILL, DONALD, in Reoch, Fowlis, testament, 1775, Comm. Dunblane. [NAS]

MCNEISH, JOHN, servant to the laird of Comrie, testament, 1676, Comm. Dunblane. [NAS]

MCNICOLL, DONALD, in Kinpauch, Blackford, testament, 1743, Comm. Dunblane. [NAS]

MCNIE, JOHN, in Innererioch, Dunning, testament, 1663, Comm. Dunblane. [NAS]

MCNIVEN, WILLIAM, a Roman Catholic and tenant of Dalclahick, Comrie, 1703. [NAS.CH1.2.5.2]

MCNUGATTOR, DONALD ROY, in Dadin, Comrie, testament, 1653, Comm. Dunblane. [NAS]

MCOMISH, DONALD, born 1727, an innkeeper in Crieff, died 1775, husband of Betty Hendry, died 1813. [Crieff MI]

MCQUEEN, ALEXANDER, from Comrie, a Jacobite imprisoned at Perth, 1746. [P.3.180]

MCRABBIE, JOHN, a Roman Catholic and officer to Lord Drummond in Auchterarder, 1703. [NAS.CH1.2.5.2]

MCRABBIE, WILLIAM, a Roman Catholic in Auchterarder, 1703. [NAS.CH1.2.52]

MCRAE, JOHN, in Cuschekachan, Comrie, testament, 1675, Comm. Dunblane. [NAS]

MCROB, CHARLES, in Lonangburn, Blackford, testament, 1669, Comm. Dunblane. [NAS]

MCROBBIE, JOHN, of Drummond, the younger, a Jacobite in 1745. [SHS.8.48]

MCRORIE, JAMES, in Muthill, 1762. [NAS.E326.1.99]

MCURICH, HELEN, in Balloch, Muthill, testament, 1768, Comm. Dunblane. [NAS]

MAILER, ANDREW, in Achterarder, a sasine, 1664. [NAS.GD160.23.10]; a burgess of Auchterarder, testament, 1689, Comm. Dunblane. [NAS]

MAILER, JOHN, born 1611, died 1696, husband of Christian More. [Kirkton of Auchterarder MI]

MAITLAND, MUNGO, factor to Murray of Abercairney, Fowlis Wester, testament, 1788, Comm. Dunblane. [NAS]

MALCOLM, DAVID, in Westmill of Auchterarder, testament, 1755, Comm. Dunblane. [NAS]

MALCOLM, GEORGE, in Loaning, Tullibardine, one of the Duke of Atholl's Fencible Men, 1706. [CAT.II]

MALCOLM, WILLIAM, in Easter Newton, Tullibardine, one of the Duke of Atholl's Fencible Men, 1706. [CAT.II]

MALCOLM, WILLIAM, born 1766, a mason in Borland Park, died 1815, husband of Jean Bayne. [Auchterarder, Main Street, MI]

MALLICE, ISABEL, spouse to John Malcolm in Clune, Auchterarder, testament, 1669, Comm. Dunblane. [NAS]

MALTMAN, WILLIAM, son of William Maltman a smith, died 1750. [Auchterarder, Aberruthven, MI]

MARSHALL, ANDREW, in Connischen, Fowlis, testament, 1652, Comm. Dunblane. [NAS]

MARSHALL, JOHN, a farmer in Dalviach, Dunning, 1797. [NAS.E326.10]

MARSHALL, ROBERT, a farmer in Dunning, 1782. [NAS.E326.1.102]

MARTIN, JOHN, in the Mains of Auchterarder, 1762. [NAS.E326.1.99]

MARTIN, JOHN, a farmer in Newton of Aberruthven, 1797. [NAS.E326.10]

MARTIN, MARGARET, born 1705, died 1744, wife of George McLeish tenant in Nether Fordon, parents of John McLeish, born 1724, died 1758. [Kirkton of Auchterarder MI]

MARTIN, PATRICK, in Dunning, testament, 1781, Comm. Dunblane. [NAS]

MASSIE, ALEXANDER, a burgess of Abernethy, testament, 1631, Comm. Dunblane. [NAS]

MATHEW, DAVID, in Glenagus, Blackford, 1762. [NAS.E326.1.99]

MATHIE, JAMES, in Aberargie, Abernethy, testament, 1737, Comm. Dunblane. [NAS]

MAULD, JANET, relict of William Oliphant in Forgandenny, testament, 1657, Comm. Dunblane. [NAS]

MAWES, JAMES, a weaver in Abernethy, testament, 1670, Comm. Dunblane. [NAS]

MAXTON, JAMES, born 1730, a farmer in Tamichnock, died 1798, father of William, born 1768, died 1797. [Fowlis Wester MI] [NAS.E326.9.2]

MAXTON, JAMES, of Cultoquhey, born 1724, died 1798, his wife Marjory Graeme, born 1745, died 1781. [Fowlis Wester MI]

MAXTON, JAMES, born 1761, a feuar in Crieff, died 1816. [Fowlis Wester MI]

MAXTON, WILLIAM, born 1715, formerly in Easter Tamichnock, Crieff, died 1782. [Fowlis Wester MI]

MEIK, JOHN, in Drinney, Fowlis, testament, 1663, Comm. Dunblane. [NAS]

MEIKLEHONNELL, PATRICK, servant to Patrick Haldane of Gleneagles, Blackford, testament, 1759, Comm. Dunblane. [NAS]

MEIKLEJOHN, JOHN, a weaver in Middle Feddal, Muthill, husband of Agnes Guild, testament, 1688, Comm. Dunblane. [NAS]

MELISS, JAMES, in Aberruchill, Comrie, testament, 1677, Comm. Dunblane. [NAS]

MENZIES, WILLIAM, and his wife Elizabeth Adie, in Middleton of Panholes, Blackford, testament, 1685, Comm. Dunblane. [NAS]

MENZIES, Mrs, in Fairntoun, Crieff, 1785. [NAS.E326.9.2]

MERCER, ROBERT, tacksman of Crieff, 1693. [NAS.GD160.199]

METHVEN, ELIZABETH, spouse to Robert Henryson in Culfargie, Abernethy, testament, 1662, Comm. Dunblane. [NAS]

MILL, PATRICK, born 1761, died 1783, son of Alexander Mill and his wife Ann Barnet in Muckarsay Mill. [Forteviot MI]

MILLER, JAMES, a tack of Over Ardoch, Muthill, 1752. [NAS.GD24.5.4.236]

MILLER, JAMES, in Tullybardine, Blackford, 1762. [NAS.E326.1.99]

MILLER, JAMES, in the Mains of Drummond, Muthill, testament, 1744, Comm. Dunblane. [NAS]

MILLAR, JAMES, born 1744, a builder in Crieff, died 1839, husband of Mary Clow, born 1776, died 1857. [Crieff MI]

MILLER, JOHN, and his wife Isobel Mushet, in Dunning, a deed, 1667. [NAS.GD220.1.C1.3.7]

MILLER, JOHN, born 1744, died 1807. [Fowlis Wester MI]

MILLER, JOHN, born 1750 in Abercairney, died 1807, husband of Isobel Kempie, born 1736, died 1803. [Fowlis Wester MI]

MILLS, PETER, born 1743, tenant of the Mill of Inverdunning, died 1801, husband of Janet Barnot, born 1737, died 1812. [Dunning MI]

MITCHELL, JAMES, tenant in Strageth, Muthill, testament, 1791, Comm. Dunblane. [NAS]

MITCHELL, MARGARET, born 1713, died 1730, daughter of John Mitchell and his wife Elizabeth Clerk. [Forteviot MI]

MITCHELL, MARY, born 1720, died 1764, wife of David Paton a flax-dresser in Crieff. [Crieff MI]

MOILL, JOHN, in Bucknie Hill, Tullibardine, one of the Duke of Atholl's Fencible Men, 1706. [CAT.II]

MOILL, WILLIAM, in Bucknie Hill, Tullibardine, one of the Duke of Atholl's Fencible Men, 1706. [CAT.II]

MOIR, ARCHIBALD, in Aberargie, testament, 1656, Comm. Dunblane. [NAS]

MOIR, JANET, heir and daughter of William Moir in Dunning, a sasine, 1665. [NAS.GD56.78]

MONCRIEFF, ALEXANDER, minister at Muckart, 1785. [NAS.E326.9.2]

MONCRIEFF, ARCHIBALD, minister at Blackford, testament, 1740, Comm. Dunblane. [NAS]

MONCRIEFF, Sir WILLIAM, minister at Blackford, 1762. [NAS.E326.1.99]

MONTEATH, JOHN, in Dunblane, 1762. [NAS.E326.1.99]

MOODIE, ROBERT, in Carrie, Abernethie, testament, 1748, Comm. Dunblane. [NAS]

MOOR, ANDREW, in Laverock Land, Tullibardine, one of the Duke of Atholl's Fencible Men, 1706. [CAT.II]

MOOR, JOHN, in Loaning, Tullibardine, one of the Duke of Atholl's Fencible Men, 1706. [CAT.II]

MORE, JAMES, in Dunning, testament, 1781, Comm. Dunblane. [NAS]

MORGONE, THOMAS, servant to Alexander Menzies of Comrie, testament, 1658, Comm. Dunblane. [NAS]

MORRIS, CATHERINE, in Auchterarder, testament, 1780, Comm. Dunblane. [NAS]

MORRIS, JAMES, a farmer in Dalviach, Dunning, 1797. [NAS.E326.10]

MORRISON, ANDREW, a maltman in Dunning, testament, 1715, Comm. Dunblane. [NAS]

MORRISON, JAMES, born 1753, a tanner in Auchterarder, died 1831, husband of Janet Imrie, born 1747, died 183, parents of Margaret and John. [Auchterarder MI]

MORRISON, PATRICK, in Monk's Croft, Tullibardine, one of the Duke of Atholl's Fencible Men, 1706. [CAT.II]

MUCKARSY, JOHN, minister at Trinity Gask, 1762. [NAS.E326.1.99]

MUDIE, ADAM, a shoemaker in Dunning, alleged to have stolen leather in 1787. [NAS.B59.31.92]

MUILL, WILLIAM, in Tullibardine, testament, 1748, Comm. Dunblane. [NAS]

MUIRHEAD, LILIAS, Lady Machany, in Blackford, testament, 1687, Comm. Dunblane. [NAS]

MULLION, ALEXANDER, born 1670, died 1732, husband of Mary Fraser, born 1679, died 1705. [Crieff MI]

MURDOCH, ANTON, in Over Gorthie, testament, 1663, Comm. Dunblane. [NAS]

MURIE, ISOBEL, relict of William Hepburn in Middle-third of Pitcairn, Dunning, testament, 1774, Comm. Dunblane. [NAS]

MURRAY, ALEXANDER, in Abernethy, 1785. [NAS.E326.9.2]

MURRAY, ANTHONY, in Crieff, 1785. [NAS.E326.9.2]

MURRAY, CHARLES, in Fowlis, 1785. [NAS.E326.9.2]

MURRAY, DANIEL, born 1742, died 1825 at Tippermallo House, husband of Catherine Miller, born 1744, died 1827. [Crieff MI]

MURRAY, DAVID, a brewer in Dunning, 1739. [NAS.CS181.7517]

MURRAY, HARRY, in Carseburn of Gleneagles, and his children Mungo and Margaret Murray, 1654. [RGS.X.241]

MURRAY, JANET, in Muthill, dead by 1688. [NAS.GD279.90]

MURRAY, MUNGO, in Alingreo, Muthill, testament, 1733, Comm. Dunblane. [NAS]

MURRAY, PATRICK, a slater in Dunning, a deed, 1703. [NAS.GD305.1.153.134]

MURRAY, WILLIAM, postmaster of Crieff, a Jacobite in 1745. [SHS.8.46]

MURRAY, Sir WILLIAM, in Barr, Monivaird, 1785. [NAS.E326.9.2]

MURRAY, ..., the younger of Dollarie, Crieff, a Jacobite in 1745. [SHS. 8.48]

NASMITH, MARGARET, daughter of Thomas Nasmith clerk to the Regality of Abernethy, testament, 1679, Comm. Dunblane. [NAS]

NEILSON, HELEN, spouse to John Mitchell in Burnbrae, Fowlis, testament, 1675, Comm. Dunblane. [NAS]

NEISH, GEORGE, a brewer in Muthill, 1762. [NAS.E326.1.99]

NICOLL, JOHN, in Fernieknowes, Dunning, testament, 1664, Comm. Dunblane. [NAS]

NIVEN, JAMES, born 1696, a weaver, died 1755. [Forteviot MI]

NIVEN, WILLIAM, born 1732, a merchant in Dunning, died 1816. [Dunning MI]

OGILVIE, ISOBEL, at Drummond, Muthill, testament, 1747, Comm. Dunblane. [NAS]

OLIPHANT, LAURENCE, the younger of Gask, a Jacobite Captain of the Perthshire Horse, 1745. [SHS.8.48]

OLIPHANT, LAURENCE, in Gask, 1785. [NAS.E326.9.2]

OLIPHANT, PATRICK, in Gask, 1739. [NAS.CS181.7517]

OLIPHANT, WILLIAM, of Carpow, Abernethy, testament, 1663, Comm. Dunblane. [NAS]

OLIPHANT, WILLIAM, of Gask, Findogask, testament, 1707, Comm. Dunblane. [NAS]

OSWALD, JAMES, in Auchterarder, testament, 1780, Comm. Dunblane. [NAS]

OSWALD, JOHN, in Loaning, Tullibardine, one of the Duke of Atholl's Fencible Men, 1706. [CAT.II]

OSWALD, JOHN, a tailor in Dunning, 1787. [NAS.B59.31.92]

OWER, JAMES, at the Mill of Gorthie, Fowlis, testament, 1667, Comm. Dunblane. [NAS]

PATERSON, ARCHIBALD, in Auchterarder, one of the Duke of Atholl's Fencible Men, 1706. [CAT.II]

PATERSON, JAMES, in Auchterarder Castle, testament, 1663, Comm. Dunblane. [NAS]

PATERSON, JAMES, in Abernethy, 1785. [NAS.E326.9.2]

PATON, FRANCIS, a farmer in Muckart, 1782. [NAS.E326.1.102]

PEARSON, WALTER, in Middlethird of Pitcairn, Dunning, testament, 1676, Comm. Dunblane. [NAS]

PEAT, AGNES, relict of Allan Hutcheson in Abernethy, testament, 1675, Comm. Dunblane. [NAS]

PEDDIE, JAMES, born 1768, a surgeon, died 1810, husband of Jean Pearson. [Auchterarder, Main Street, MI][NAS.GD59.38.5.22]

PENNY, JOHN, in Aberruthven, testament, 1781, Comm. Dunblane. [NAS]

PENNEY, JOHN, late servant to James Craig a farmer in Strathy, Auchterarder, was apprenticed to Thomas Brown a weaver in Perth, 1784. [NAS.B59.29.172]

PERNIE, JOHN, in Cairnhead, Blackford, testament, 1668, Comm. Dunblane. [NAS]

PETRIE, COLIN, in Auchterarder, a letter, 1729. [NAS.CH12.23.75]

PHILIP, JOHN, of Cowden, Comrie, testament, 1747, Comm. Dunblane. [NAS]

PHILP, Mrs, in Coudan, Muthill, 1762. [NAS.E326.1.99]

PILMAR, PETER, minister at Forgandenny, a letter, 1735. [NAS.B59.28.106]

PITCAIRN, ELIZABETH, daughter of Andrew Pitcairn portioner of Abernethy, testament, 1754, Comm. Dunblane. [NAS]

PITKEATHLIE, JOHN, a tack of Braefoot of Rossie, Forgandenny, 1759. [NAS.GD1.391.55]

PITKEATHLIE, MARGARET, spouse of Thomas Flockhart, in Thainsland, Dunning, testament, 1604, Comm. Dunblane. [NAS]

PITTINBROG, BEATRIX, spouse of William Imbrie in Aberargie, testament, 1616, Comm. Dunblane. [NAS]

POLLOCK, WILLIAM, in Milton of Auchterarder, testament, 1727, Comm. Dunblane. [NAS]

PORTEOUS, JAMES, moderator of the Presbytery of Auchterarder, 1744. [NAS.CH1.2.84.FO.63]

PORTEOUS, MARY, born 1775, died 1803, wife of James Clemen a wright in Crieff. [Crieff MI]

PROUDFOOT, MARGARET, in Methven, testament, 1659, Comm. Dunblane. [NAS]

RAEBURN, JOHN, in Tullibardine, testament, 1679, Comm. Dunblane. [NAS]

RAMSAY, ANDREW, in Gorthie, testament, 1664, Comm. Dunblane. [NAS]

RANKINE, JAMES, in Middletown of Gask, testament, 1748, Comm. Dunblane. [NAS]

REID, JAMES, minister at Gask, 1762. [NAS.E326.1.99]

REID, JOHN, in Auchterarder, testament, 1771, Comm. Dunblane. [NAS]

RENNY, ARCHIBALD, minister at Muckart, 1782. [NAS.E326.1.102]

RICHARD, ISOBEL, in Drumdowie, Muthill, testament, 1681, Comm. Dunblane. [NAS]

RICHARDSON, JAMES, in Forgandenny, testament, 1658, Comm. Dunblane. [NAS]

RIDDOCH, JOHN, in Cultabraggan, Comrie, testament, 1767, Comm. Dunblane. [NAS]

RIDDOCH, WILLIAM, a Roman Catholic and tacksman of Garrichow, Comrie, 1703. [NAS.CH1.2.5.2]

RINTOUL, ALEXANDER, born 1761, farmer at East Oswald, died 1828. [Fowlis Wester MI]

RINTOUL, WILLIAM, portioner of Abernehy, testament, 1723, Comm. Dunblane. [NAS]

RITCHARD, JAMES, in Middle Third, Tullibardine, one of the Duke of Atholl's Fencible Men, 1706. [CAT.II]

RITCHARD, JOHN, in Milne, Tullibardine, one of the Duke of Atholl's Fencible Men, 1706. [CAT.II]

RITCHIE, ROBERT, in Fowlis, testament, 1719, Comm. Dunblane. [NAS]

ROBERTSON, JAMES, a tenant farmer in Heatherlaye, died 1759, husband of Isobel Horn, born 1712, died 1788. [Arngask MI]

ROBERTSON, JOHN, a merchant in Blackford, testament, 1781, Comm. Dunblane. [NAS]

ROBIN, THOMAS, in Drumqhair, Muthill, testament, 1679, Comm. Dunblane. [NAS]

RODGIE, JOHN, born 1693, died in Craigentore 1747. [Fowlis Wester MI]

ROLLO, ANDREW, a tailor in Pottie, Abernethy, testament, 1686, Comm. Dunblane. [NAS]

ROLLO, Captain, in Dunning, 1782. [NAS.E326.1.102]

RONALD, JANET, spouse to Alexander Pearson in Clow, Dunning, testament, 1676, Comm. Dunblane. [NAS]

ROSS, ELIZABETH, in Dunning, testament, 1781, Comm. Dunblane. [NAS]

ROSS, JOHN, a student, son of James Ross minister at Forteviot, 1618. [NAS.B59.28.22]

ROY, JAMES, in Aberdalgie, 1785. [NAS.326.9.2]

ROY, NEIL, in Laverock Land, Tullibardine, one of the Duke of Atholl's Fencible Men, 1706. [CAT.II]

ROY, WILLIAM, in Auchterarder, testament, 1780, Comm. Dunblane. [NAS]

RUTHERFORD, DUNCAN, born 1763, died 1834, husband of Janet Dougall, born 1762, died 1834. [Forteviot MI]

RUTHERFORD, JOHN, in Nether Gask, testament, 1663, Comm. Dunblane. [NAS]

RYDER, JAMES, in Inverpeffrey, testament, 1733, Comm. Dunblane. [NAS]

SCOBIE, JAMES, in Aquhaick, Blackford, testament, 1672, Comm. Dunblane. [NAS]

SCOTT, BARBARA, born 1754, died 1810, wife of Peter Don a shoemaker in Crieff. [Crieff MI]

SCOTT, DAID, in Ramore, Abernethy, testament, 1731, Comm. Dunblane. [NAS]

SCOTT, DUNCAN, born 1757, died 1814. [Fowlis Wester MI]

SCOTT, JAMES, minister at Muthill, 1762. [NAS.E326.1.99]

SETON, or MCGREGOR, DONALD, in Glenmuik, Comrie, testament, 1711, Comm. Dunblane. [NAS]

SETON, JOHN, born 1747, a nurseryman in Crieff, died 1801. [Crieff MI]

SHAIRP, DAVID, a tenant on the lands of Dalreoch and Balgour, parish of Dunning, 1695. [NAS.GD56.128]

SHARP, ANDREW, in Milntown, Tullibardine, one of the Duke of Atholl's Fencible Men, 1706. [CAT.II]

SHARP, MARGARET, daughter of John Sharp in Hillhead of Machany, spouse of Patrick Richard in Carlaveroch, Muthill, testament, 1759 Comm. Dunblane. [NAS]

SHEDDAN, JAMES, feuar and merchant in Auchterarder, testament, 1756, Comm. Dunblane. [NAS]

SHEDDAN, MUNGO, in Auchterarder, a deed, 1733. [NAS.GD38.1.796]

SHEWENGER, PATRICK, in Abernethy, testament, Comm. Dunblane, 1681. [NAS]

SHIOCH, JANET, in Aberdalgie, testament,

1754, Comm. Dunblane. [NAS]

SHOOLBRAIDS, JANET, spouse to Andrew Geddes in Carpow, testament, 1672 Comm. Dunblane. [NAS]

SINCLAIR, DONALD, in Muthill, testament,

1781, Comm. Dunblane. [NAS]

SINCLAIR, JOHN, in Loaning, Tullibardine, one of the Duke of Atholl's Fencible Men, 1706. [CAT.II]

SIRES, WILLIAM, in Aberargie, testament,

1622, Comm. Dunblane. [NAS]

SKEALOCH, JAMES, in Kinlochan, Comrie, testament, 1665, Comm. Dunblane. [NAS]

SLEGER, MARY, a Roman Catholic in Conuke, Auchterarder, 1703. [NAS.CH1.2.5.2]

SMALL, ANDREW, in West Dron, 1701. [NAS.GD305.1.153.78]

SMALL, JOHN, and his wife Christian Lyall in Aberagie, Abernethy, testament, 1687, Comm. Dunblane. [NAS]

SMART, JAMES, in Allichmoir, Muthill, testament, 1675, Comm. Dunblane. [NAS]

SMEATON, DAVID, in Pitcairn, Dunning, testament, 1686 Comm. Dunblane. [NAS]

SMITH, ALEXANDER, minister at Dunning, testament, 1771, Comm. Dunblane. [NAS]

SMITH, DAVID, in Methven, 1785. [NAS.E326.9.2]

SMITH, PATRICK, of Braco, 163. [NAS.GD190.1.5]; a land grant in the Barony of Geneagles, 1658. [RGS.X.661]

SMITH, WILLIAM, from Drummond, Muthill, a Jacobite in 1745. [SHS. 8.50]

SMITTON, ANDREW, in Auchterarder, 1762. [NAS.E326.1.99]

SMITTON, JOHN, of Broadfold, born 1736, a farmer at West Kirkton, died 1815, husband of Helen Fenton, born 1751, died 1818. [Kirkton of Auchterhouse MI]

SMITTON, PATRICK, born 1723, a farmer at West Kirkton, died 1785. [Kirkton of Auchterarder MI]

SMITTON, PETER, of Holtoun, born 1718, died 1794, husband of (1) Susanna George, born 1721, died 1757, (2) Elizabeth Ritchie, born 1734, died 1760. [Kirkton of Auchterarder MI]

SMYTON, JOHN, died 1706. [Kirkton of Auchterarder MI]

SOMMERVILLE, WILLIAM, in Rhynd, 1785. [NAS.E326.9.2]

SORLIE, JAMES, in Bucknie Hill, Tullibardine, one of the Duke of Atholl's Fencible Men, 1706. [CAT.II]

SORLIE, JOHN, in West Park Tullibardine, one of the Duke of Atholl's Fencible Men, 1706. [CAT.II]

SPREULL, JAMES, in Abernethy, testament, 1611, Comm. Dunblane. [NAS]

STALKER, ANDREW, in Park, Tullibardine, one of the Duke of Atholl's Fencible Men, 1706. [CAT.II]

STALKER, THOMAS, gardener at Innerpeffrey, Muthill, testament, 1728 Comm. Dunblane. [NAS]

STEEDMAN, MICHAEL, in Dunning, testament, 1781, Comm. Dunblane. [NAS]

STEVEN, MARGARET, spouse to William Cunningham in Abernethy, testament, 1680, Comm. Dunblane. [NAS]

STEWART, JAMES, from Drummond, Muthill, a Jacobite in 1745. [SHS. 8.52]

STEWART, JANET, born 1777, daughter of John Stewart of Innerdunning, wife of John Laing a skipper in Grangemouth, died 1816. [Auchterarder, Main Street, MI]

STEWART, JOHN, of Innerdunning, born 1732, died 1820, husband of Margaret Chalmers, born 1749, died 1832. [Auchterarder, Main Street, MI]

STEWART, WILLIAM, from Drummond, Muthill, a Jacobite in 1745. [SHS.8.52]

STEWART, WILLIAM, born 1698, died 1742, husband of Janet Henderson, born 1700, died 1775. [Dunning MI]

STIRLING, Sir HARRY, of Ardoch, Blackford, testament, 1670, Comm.Dunblane. [NAS]

STIRLING, ROBERT, born 1740, minister at Crieff, died 1813, husband of Margaret Drummond, born 1752, died 1826. [Crieff MI]

STIRLING, Sir WILLIAM, in Muthill, 1762; 1785. [NAS.E326.1.99; 9.2]

STIRLING, WILLIAM, in Dunblane, 1762; 1785. [NAS.E326.1.99; 9.2]

STOBIE, WILLIAM, in Fowlis, testament, 1683, Comm.Dunblane. [NAS]

STRACHAN, JOHN, in Baldinnis, Dunning, testament, 1685, Comm.Dunblane. [NAS]

STRATHIE, ALEXANDER, a cordiner in Machany, Blackford, testament, 1663, Comm.Dunblane. [NAS]

STRATHIE, JOHN, in Easthill, Tullibardine, one of the Duke of Atholl's Fencible Men, 1706. [CAT.II]

SUNZEOUR, THOMAS, in Easter Cluny, Abernethy, testament, 1684, Comm.Dunblane. [NAS]

SWINTON, ROBERT, in Keathliehead, Auchterarder, testament, 1685, Comm.Dunblane. [NAS]

SWORD, JAMES, in Abercairnie, Fowlis, testament, 1677, Comm.Dunblane. [NAS]

SYME, ANN, in Auchterarder, testament, 1781, Comm.Dunblane. [NAS]

SYMMIE, ELSPETH, in Easter Keillour, Fowlis, testament, 1664, Comm.Dunblane. [NAS]

TAINS, ISOBEL, a Roman Catholic in Drummond, Auchterarder, 1703. [NAS.CH1.2.5.2]

TAINSH, JOHN, aborn 1728, a vintner in Crieff, died 1784. [Crieff MI]

TAISH, JOHN, in Culwhatock, Muthill, testament, 1673, Comm.Dunblane. [NAS]

TAYLOR, BATHIA, born 1731, died 1784, wife of Alexander Graham in East Mill of Gorthy. [Fowlis Wester MI]

TAYLOR, DAVID, in Auchterarder, testament, 1681, Comm.Dunblane. [NAS]

TAYLOR, GEORGE, from Muthill, a Jacobite in 1745. [P.3.364]

TAYLOR, JOHN, born 1711, a merchant in Crieff, died 1789. [Crieff MI]

THOMSON, JOHN, a schoolmaster in Muthill, around 1770, a letter, 1783.[NAS.E177.103; GD190.3.332]

THOMSON, WILLIAM, a cordiner in Abernethy, testament, 1664, Comm.Dunblane. [NAS]

TOD, DAVID, a weaver in Burnside of West Dron, Abernethy, testament, 1676, Comm.Dunblane. [NAS]

TOSCHEOCH, CHRISTIAN, in Machany, Blackford, testament, 1677, Comm.Dunblane. [NAS]

TYRIE, JOHN, a litster burgess of Perth, was granted the lands of Busbies in the lordship of Methven on 3 January 1654. [RGS.X.228]

WADDELL, JAMES, in Duchaly, Blackford, testament, 1736, Comm.Dunblane. [NAS]

WALKER, DUNCAN, in Drummond, testament, 1674, Comm.Dunblane. [NAS]

WARDLAW, MARGARET, in Dunning, testament, 1781, Comm.Dunblane. [NAS]

WATSON, ANDREW, in Petindo, Abernethy, testament, 1774, Comm.Dunblane. [NAS]

WATSON, ROBERT, in Aberdalgie, 1785. [NAS.E326.9.2]

WATT, JAMES, a miller, died 1674. [Fowlis Wester MI]

WEBSTER, ROBERT, in Fowlis, 1785. [NAS.E326.9.2]

WEDDERSPOON, DAVID, born 1728, a wright, died 1800, husband of Margaret ......, born 1746, died 1789. [Crieff MI]

WEDDERSPOON, DAVID, tenant in Dalnydragon, died 1807, husband of Elizabeth Robertson, died 1814. [Fowlis Wester MI]

WEDDERSPOON, WILLIAM, in Caldside, Abernethy, testament, 1731, Comm.Dunblane. [NAS]

WEMYSS, GILBERT, in Abernethy, testament, 1662, Comm.Dunblane. [NAS]

WEMYSS,MUNGO, minister at Aberdalgie, testament, 1670, Comm.Dunblane. [NAS]

WHYTE, JOHN, a farmer in Forteviot, 1782. [NAS.E326.1.102]

WILSON, DAVID, born 1749, a tenant in Forteviot, died 1786, husband of Helen Mitchell, born 1764, died 1786. [Forteviot MI]

WILSON, WILLIAM, in Easter Moncrieff, late at Bridge of Earn, sasine, 1685. [NAS.GD1.157.1]

WILTER, THOMAS, an artist in Muthill, 1749. [NAS.B59.36.17]

WINTON, ROBERT, died 1737. [Dunning MI]

WOODERSPOON, DAVID, born 1709, a wright and feuar in Crieff, died 1761, husband of Ann Sharp, born 1711, died 1790, parents of John Wooderspon, born 1740, late of the Mains of Dargall, died 1802. [Crieff MI]

WORKMAN, JOHN, in Keillour, Fowlis, testament, 1604, Comm.Dunblane. [NAS]

WRIGHT, MARGARET, spouse of Andrew Mailer, in Auchterarder, a deed, 1676. [NAS.GD160.23.11]

YOUNG, JOHN, born 1677, died 1747. [Forteviot MI]

YOUNG, Mrs MARGARET, in Colquilzie, Muthill, 1762. [NAS.E326.1.99]

YOUNG, THOMAS, in Dunning, testament, 1781, Comm.Dunblane. [NAS]

REFERENCES

CAT = Chronicles of Atholl and Tullibardine Families, [Edinburgh 1908]

NAS =   National Archives of Scotland, Edinburgh

NLS =   National Library of Scotland, Edinburgh

P   =   Prisoners of the '45, [Edinburgh, 1929]

SHS =   Scottish History Society

TNA =   National Archives, London

ABBREVIATIONS

Comm.   =   Commissariat

MI   =   Monumental Inscription

ABBOT, PATRICK, a parishioner of Alyth, 1651. [HA#95]

ADAM, JAMES, servant to William Fell a hammerman in Meigle, 1726. [NAS.GD68.1.300]

ADAM, JOHN, an Elder of Alyth parish, 1650. [HA#83]

ADAM, THOMAS, a smith in Meigle, testament, 30 June 1726, Comm. Dunkeld. [NAS]

ADAM, WALTER, in Parckie, Meigle, testament, 26 July 1771, Comm. Dunkeld. [NAS]

ADAMSON, ALEXANDER, a wright in Alyth, a bond, 1683. [NAS.RD4.52.524]

ADAMSON, JOHN, in Kirkton of Rattray, a bond, 1672. [NAS.RD4.31.452]

AITKEN, WILLIAM, in Coupar Angus, a witness to a sasine, 1698. [NAS.GD68/1/26B]

ALEXANDER, JAMES, tenant of Kinkedly etc, Alyth, 1790. [NAS.GD83.I. 737]

ALEXANDER, PATRICK, in Ballendoch, Alyth, testament, 22 September 1714, Comm. Dunkeld. [NAS]

ALEXANDER, THOMAS, husband of Marjory McDougall, died pre 1796, parents of James, Thomas, and Alexander in Kinkedly. [Alyth MI]

ALEXANDER, WILLIAM, in Alyth, a deed, 1702. [NAS.RD4.90.582]

ALLAN, JOHN, sometime in Easter Craig, thereafter in Alyth, testament, 30 November 1752, Comm. Dunkeld. [NAS]

ANDERSON, ANN, wife of John Mitchell in Berryhillock, died 1746. [Blairgowrie MI]

ANDERSON, JOHN, portioner of the Kirkton of Rattray, born 1627, died 1682. [Rattray MI]

ANDERSON, JOHN, minister at Cargill, letters, 1629. [NAS.GD8.667]

ANDERSON, JOHN, tenant of Bastardbank, tack of Newton of Bamff plus land formerly part of Fyall farm, Alyth, 1790. [NAS.GD83.I.736]

ANDERSON, WILLIAM, in Alyth, 1653. [HA#96]

ARCHER, ANDREW, sometime tenant in Broomhill, thereafter in Coupar Angus, testament, 20 March 1775, Comm. Dunkeld. [NAS]

ARCHER, PATRICK, died 1753, husband of Helen Bowman, died 1750. [Meigle MI]

ARROT, JAMES, an Elder of Alyth parish, 1653. [HA#93]

ARTHUR, ELIZABETH, born 1681, wife of William Soutar in Murgunstoun, died 1728. [Blairgowrie MI]

ARTHUR, JOHN, born 1597, died 1662, portioner of Middlemaws. [Blairgowrie MI]

AUCHTERLAUNY, JAMES, born 1661, died 1685. [Meigle MI]

AYTON, THOMAS, minister of Alyth from 1720 to 1735. [F.V.250]

BALFOUR, ANDREW, a Deacon of Alyth parish, 1655. [HA#93/98]

BANKS, JOHN, born 1751, a merchant in Coupar Angus, died 1787, husband of Elizabeth Duncan, born 1744, died 1803. [Coupar Angus MI]

BARCLAY, JOHN, minister of Meigle from 1609 to 1622, husband of Eliza Halliburton, parents of James, John, and Margaret. [F.V.270]

BARNET, JAMES, in Coupar Grange, testament, 19 March 1736, Comm. Dunkeld. [NAS]

BARNET, WILLIAM, in Alyth, testament, 21 February 1688, Comm. Dunkeld. [NAS]

BAXTER, HUGH, a student of divinity, late in Blairgowrie, testament, 14 January 1784, Comm. St Andrews. [NAS]

BAXTER, JOHN, in Drumloch, born 1638, died 1691, husband of Marjory Young, born 1648, died 1698. [Blairgowrie MI]

BAXTER, JOHN, sometime in Alyth, testament, 20 September 1770, Comm. Dunkeld. [NAS]

BAXTER, JOHN, at Bleachfield of Balharry, parish of Alyth, testament, 11 June 1779, Comm. Dunkeld. [NAS]

BEILL, ANDREW, born 1587, died 1650, husband of Elisabeth, in Batterwall. [Meigle MI]

BELL, JOHN, born 1729, gardener at Belmont Castle, died 1784, wife Elizabeth, born 1730, died 1811. [Meigle MI]

BELL, JOHN, sr., a wright in Coupar Angus, testament, 14 March 1749, Comm. Dunkeld. [NAS]

BENNET, ROBERT, husband of Marjory Morson (born 1665, died 1710), at the Boat of Blair. [Rattray MI]

BITTER, ISOBELL, a recusant in Alyth, 1655. [HA#98]

BLACK, JAMES and JOHN, tenants in Myde and Drumglay, parish of Blairgowrie, 1791. [NAS.GD83/742]

BLAIR, ANDREW, and his wife Elizabeth Kae at the Mill of Camno, parents of Agnes, born 1680, died 1695, and Elspeth, 1683-1690. [Meigle MI]

BLAIR, GILBERT, minister of Blairgowrie from 1688 to 1701, died after 1731. [F.V.256]

BLAIR, JOHN, in Blacklaw, born 1628, died 1681. [Rattray MI]

BLAIR, THOMAS, schoolmaster of Blairgowrie, a bond, 1676. [NAS.RD3.42.374]

BLAIR, THOMAS, born 1636, son of Thomas Blair of Ardblair, minister of Blairgowrie 1664 to 1688, minister of Bendochy from 1688 to his death in 1692, husband of Helen Malcolm, parents of William, Margaret, Isabel and Helen, [F.V.253/256]; bonds, 1681, 1701. [NAS.RD4.49.23, etc; RD4.89.585]

BLAIR, WILLIAM, born around 1591, minister of Eassie and Nevay from 1616 to 1617. [F.V.259]

BLAIR, WILLIAM, a shoemaker in Rattray, testament, 7 October 1740, Comm. Dunkeld. [NAS]

BOWES, ROBERT, minister of Rattray, testament, 21 February 1751, Comm. Dunkeld. [NAS]

BROW, ANDREW, in Alyth, 1655. [HA#96]

BROWN, EUPHAN, born 1686, died 1715, wife of Patrick Thomson miller at the Mill of Meigle. [Meigle MI]

BROWN, DAVID, minister of Eassie and Nevay from 1617 to 1635. [F.V. 259]

BROWN, GEORGE, born 1673, a farmer in Sachar, died 1744, husband of Janet Lownie. [Meigle MI]

BROWN, GEORGE, a merchant in Blairgowrie, 1792. [NAS.CS228/ B8/21]

BRUCE, GEORGE, portioner of Coupar Angus, testament, 18 August 1748, Comm. Dunkeld. [NAS]

BRUCE, THOMAS, in Coupar Angus, testament, 3 December 1728, Comm. Dunkeld. [NAS]

BRUCE, THOMAS, an elder of Coupar Angus, 1775. [NAS.CH2.395.6/8]

BRUCE, THOMAS, born 1724, a merchant in Coupar Angus, died in January 1803, husband of Janet Simpson who died in August 1781. [Coupar Angus MI]

BRYDIE, JAMES, in Bonnyton of Rattray, a bond, 1676. [NAS.RD4.40.135]

BURMAN, ANDREW, a writer and notary in Coupar Angus, father of John Burman, bonds and deeds, 1681,1685, 1687, 1692; 1697; witness to a sasine, 1698. [NAS.RD2.54.540; RD2.61.121; RD2.68.662/1352; RD4.60.259; RD2.75.87; RD2.81/1.137; GD68/1/26B]

BURNMAN, JOHN, in Coupar Angus, testament, 21 July 1781, Comm. Dunkeld. [NAS]

BUTTER, GEORGE, in Blair, relict Christian Ballentyne, testament, 1691, Comm. St Andrews. [NAS]

BUTTER, JANET, a parishioner of Coupar Angus, 1775. [NAS.CH2.395.6/6]

CAMPBELL, ALEXANDER, a merchant in Alyth, testament, 30 March 1758, Comm. Dunkeld. [NAS]

CAMPBELL, DAVID, of Kethick, 1719. [NAS.GD83.I.615/616/617]

CAMPBELL, GEORGE, a flesher in Coupar Angus, testament, 16 December 1740, Comm. Dunkeld. [NAS]

CAMPBELL, GEORGE, a flesher in Coupar Angus, testament, 7 December 1784, Comm. Dunkeld. [NAS]

CAMPBELL, ISOBEL, widow of David Fleming, in Easter Bleatoun, Rattray, testament, 22 May 1759, Comm. Dunkeld. [NAS]

CAMPBELL, PATRICK, of Keithock, 1611. [NAS.GD68.1.136]

CANT, WILLIAM, in Alyth, testament, 21 June 1690, Comm. Dunkeld. [NAS]

CARGILL, DONALD, notary and vicar of Rattray, father of John Cargill, 1622. [NAS.GD68.1.164]

CARGILL, DONALD, in Alyth, 1669. [HA#116]

CARGILL, DONALD, of Halton of Rattray, bonds, 1672, 1673, 1675. [NAS.RD4.31.452; RD4.33.494; RD4.37.169]

CARGILL, DONALD, son of John Cargill, in Blairgowrie, a bond, 1676. [NAS.RD4.39.694]

CARGILL, HENRY, a merchant in Alyth, 1637. [NAS.GD68.1.193]

CARGILL, JAMES, in Alyth, 1665. [HA#97]

CARGILL, JAMES, in Bonytoun of Rattray, bonds, 1675. [NAS.RD4.37.169; RD2.39.607]

CARGILL, JAMES, in Halton of Rattray, bonds of corrobation/bonds, 1675, 1676,1678, 1679. [NAS.RD4.38.79; RD3.43.386; RD3.44.354; RD3.45.58; CS181.974]

CARGILL, JAMES, only son of the late David Cargill, a feuar in Alyth, a disposition, 1791. [NAS.GD16.12.69]

CARGILL, JOHN, notary of the Diocese of Dunkeld, eldest son of Donald Cargill, notary in the Kirkton of Rattray, 1612. [NAS.GD68.1.141/142]

CARGILL, JOHN, a weaver in Coupar Angus, testament, 9 May 1786, Comm. Dunkeld. [NAS]

CARGILL, LAURENCE, in Kirkton of Rattray, a sasine, 1644; a bond of corrobation, 1679. [NAS.GD68.1.202; RD3.45.55]

CARGILL, MARGARET, spouse of James Cargill in Newton of Bamff, Alyth, testament, 5 April 1690, Comm. Dunkeld. [NAS]

CARGILL, WILLIAM, in Rattray, testament, 29 November 1701, Comm. Dunkeld. [NAS]

CHALMERS, ANDREW, of Alrie, a flesher in Alyth,testament, 31 August 1727, Comm. Dunkeld. [NAS]

CHALMERS, GEORGE, tenant of Hatton and Mains Moss, parish of Blairgowrie, 1800. [NAS.GD83/1068]

CHALMERS, JAMES, eldest son of William Chalmers a writer in Alyth, a disposition, 1769. [NAS.GD83.I.381]

CHALMERS, JAMES, in Pedrey, a Deacon of Alyth parish, 1638. [HA#67]

CHALMERS, JOHN, a merchant in Alyth, testament, 21 June 1784, Comm. Dunkeld. [NAS]

CHALMERS, MARGARET, in Alyth, testament, 28 November 1765, Comm. Dunkeld. [NAS]

CHAPMAN, ANDREW, a litster in Coupar Angus, a deed, 1727. [NAS.RS2.94.570]

CHAPMAN, ANDREW, late brewer in Coupar Angus, testament, 6 August 1754, Comm. Dunkeld. [NAS]

CHRYSTIESON, PATRICK, a surgeon in Coupar Angus, testaments, 24 May 1720 and 22 May 1753, Comm. Dunkeld. [NAS]

CLARK, DAVID, a chapman in Coupar Angus, testament, 29 November 1701, Comm. Dunkeld. [NAS]

CLARK, DAVID, a vintner in Coupar Angus, was admitted as a burgess of St Andrews on 15 November 1738. [St Andrews Burgh Court Book]

CLESSON, THOMAS, an Elder of Alyth, 1674. [HA#108]

CLYDE, MARGARET, relict of George Herring kirk officer of Rattray, testament, 12 August 1762, Comm. Dunkeld. [NAS]

COCHRANE, GEORGE, in Mains of Kirkhill, Meigle, testament, 7 April 1690, Comm. Dunkeld. [NAS]

COGHORN, AGNES, in Alyth, 1650. [HA#82]

COLVILLE, MARGARET, relict of James Pringle an apothecary in Coupar Angus, and spouse of William Lyon of Easter Ogil, a deed, 1696. [NAS.RD4.79.328]

COPPER, JAMES, born 1612, died 1685, husband of Agnes Low, born 1622, died 1702, indwellers in Blackfold of Fullarton. [Meigle MI]

CRANSTON, ROBERT, a soldier in Germany and Poland, returned to Scotland, later Bishop of Dunkeld, died in 1685. [Meigle MI]

CRICHTON, DAVID, servant to John Smith, a writer in Leitfie, 1726. [NAS.GD68.1.300]

CRICHTON, DAVID, portioner of the Mains of Rattray, father of Magdalene, a bond, 1730. [NAS.GD83.I.619]

CRICHTON, DAVID, a merchant in Alyth, financial records, 1793-1820. [NAS.CS96.322.1/2/3]

CRICHTON, EUPHEMIA, in Coupar Angus, testament, 14 February 1776, Comm. Dunkeld. [NAS]

CRICHTON, GEORGE, in the Mains of Rattray, testament, 15 July 1751, Comm. Dunkeld. [NAS]

CRICHTON, JAMES, in Coupar Angus, bonds, 1677. [NAS.RD4.40.595; RD4.41.652]

CRICHTON, ROBERT, minister of Eassie and Nevay from 1637 to his death in 1665. [F.V.259]

CRICHTON, THOMAS, in Barmenie, an Elder of Alyth parish, 1638. [HA#67]

CROCKATT, DONALD, bailie of Alyth, 1654. [HA#102]

CROCKATT, DONALD, in Kirkton of Rattray, a bond, 1679. [NAS.RD4.45.83]

CROCKATT, JAMES, son of George Crockatt in Coupar Angus, a physician who settled in Charleston, South Carolina, by 1752, died there on 16 April 1765. [NAS.RD4.178.252; S/H.18.5.1763]

CROCKATT, GEORGE, a surgeon in Coupar Angus, testament, 26 October 1763, Comm. Dunkeld. [NAS]

CROCKATT, JAMES, of Easter Rattray, bonds/tack/deeds, 1673, 1675, 1676, 1677, 1679, 1688. [NAS.RD3.34.527; RD4.38.373; RD2.41.182; RD4.40.701; RD4.46.125; RD4.63.120]

CROCKATT, JOHN, a Deacon of Alyth parish, 1655. [HA#93]

CROCKATT, JOHN, in Bairdmonie, an Elder of Alyth, 1671. [HA#108]

CROCKATT, JOHN, son of James Crockatt of Easter Rattray, bonds, 1669, 1673, 1674, 1675, 1676, 1677, 1679, 1681, 1690; deeds, 1685, 1688, 1701, 1702. [NAS.RD3.21.153, RD4.33.400; RD4.34.716; RD4.35.320; RD4.38.373; RD3.63.258; RD2.41.182; RD4.46.125; RD2.43.780; RD4.48.800, etc; RD4.63.120; RD4.65.1016; RD4.89.720; RD4.90.1021]

CROCKATT, JOHN, a writer in Coupar Angus, a deed, 1685. [NAS.RD4.56.62]

CROCKATT, JOHN, in Easter Letfie, Alyth, bailie of Airlie, testament, 29 November 1782, Comm. Dunkeld. [NAS]

CROCKATT, MARJORIE, relict of James Ogilvie bailie of Alyth, testament, 18 November 1725, Comm. Dunkeld. [NAS]

CROCKATT, PATRICK, in Alyth, bonds, 1674, 1676, a deed, 1685. [NAS.RD4.35.453; RD4.39.55.]

CROOKSHANKS, JAMES, a flesher in Coupar Angus, testaments, 29 August 1716 and 17 December 1717, Comm. Dunkeld. [NAS]

CROOKSHANK, THOMAS, in Coupar Angus, bailie for James Laird of Bendoch, 1726. [NAS.GD68.1.300]

CULROSS, HELEN, in Alyth, 1667. [HA#97]

CUNNINGHAM, WILLIAM, born 1630, died 1688, husband of Janet Hay, born 1638, died 1681. [Meigle MI]

DALGAIRN, JOHN, a brewer in Meigle, died 1728, husband of Margaret Christie, born 1677, died 1727, parents of John, Alexander, and William. [Meigle MI]

DALGARDNO, WILLIAM, schoolmaster and Session Clerk of Alyth, 1653-1656. [HA#94]

DAVIDSON, ADAM, born 1679, minister of Eassie and Nevay from 1702 to his death on 20 October 1720, husband of Agnes Slows or Thomson. [F.V.260]

DEFFERS, DAVID, a bleacher in West Mill of Rattray, testament, 16 April 1776, Comm. Dunkeld. [NAS]

DEUCHAR, JOHN, tack of Craighead, Alyth, 1797. [NAS.GD83.I.748]

DICK, EUPHAM, in Clayhills, Rattray, testament, 9 January 1752, Comm. Dunkeld. [NAS]

DICK, GEORGE, died in December 1764, father of William, Thomas, James and Allen. [Alyth MI]

DICK, WILLIAM, an apothecary in Alyth, deeds, 1701, 1702; testaments, 27 June 1713 and 3 June 1721, Comm. Dunkeld. [NAS.RD4.88.227; RD4.90.582]

DICK, WILLIAM, a vintner in Alyth, a disposition, 1791. [NAS.GD16.12.69]

DICKSON, ISABEL, born 1650, died 1724, wife of John Anderson, parents of Ann. [Blairgowrie MI]

DICKSON, LAURANCE, in Halton of Rattray, testament, 1684, Comm. Dunkeld. [NAS]

DOIG, ROBERT, born 1612, died 1651, husband of Isobel Tylar in Mains of Meigle, [Meigle MI]

DON, ALEXANDER, in Alyth, a deed, 1702. [NAS.RD4.90.582]

DONALD, DAVID, of Shangrie, Alyth, 1666. [HA#98]

DONALDSON, DAVID, portioner of the Mains of Rattray, a deed, 1689. [NAS.RD2.70.478]; in Cotyards, born 1630, died 1715. [Rattray MI]

DONALDSON, JAMES, son of John Donaldson, in Kirkton of Rattray, a heritable bond, 1682; testament, 7 November 1699, Comm. Dunkeld. [NAS.RD4.51.573]

DONALDSON, JAMES, portioner of the Mains of Rattray, born 1585, died 1659. [Rattray MI]

DONALDSON, JOHN, son of John Donaldson, in Kirkton of Rattray, heritable bonds, 1675, 1682. [NAS.RD4.37.407; RD4.51.573]; a writer in Rattray, testament, 11 June 1696, Comm. Dunkeld. [NAS]

DONALDSON, JOHN, of Bonnyton of Rattray, born 1659, died 1732, husband of Marjory Ireland, born 1673, died 1739. [Rattray MI]

DONALDSON, PATRICK, son of John Donaldson, in Kirkton of Rattray, a heritable bond, 1682. [NAS.RD4.51.573]

DOUGALL, ANDREW, tenant in Arthurstone, Coupar Angus, testament, 29 November 1782, Comm. Dunkeld. [NAS]

DOW, MARGARET, in Coupar Angus, relict of Andrew Scott, testament, 15 November 1800, Comm. Dunkeld. [NAS]

DOW, WILLIAM, minister of Blairgowrie from 1769 to 1786, husband of Mary Duncan, parents of Ann, Andrew, Patrick, Robert, William, Grace, and John. [F.V.256]

DOW, WILLIAM, son of Reverend Dow in Blairgowrie, died in Antigua on 7 July 1803. [AJ#2907][EEC#14316][GM#73.882]

DRUMMOND, DONALD, of Kirkton of Rattray, husband of Catherine Sanders, relict of James Soutar in Blair, a tack, 1672. [NAS.RD3.30.315]

DRUMMOND, JAMES, in Kirkton of Rattray, a deed. 1692. [NAS.RD4.71.15]

DRUMMOND, JOHN, of Blairgowrie, a deed, 1690. [NAS.RD3.73.66]

DRUMMOND, JOHN, in Coupar Angus, testaments, 2 August 1695 and 16 January 1696, Comm. Dunkeld. [NAS]

DRUMMOND, PATRICK, in Rattray, testament, 17 November 1725, Comm. Dunkeld. [NAS]

DRUMMOND, WILLIAM, in Burnhead of Blairgowrie, a bond, 1669. [NAS.RD4.23.254]

DUKE, JOHN, a butcher in Coupar Angus, imprisoned as a suspected Jacobite 1746-1747. [P.2.168]

DUFFUS, DAVID, born 1728, a manufacturer and bleacher, died at Haugh of Rattray in 1773, husband of Helen Mitchell, born 1729, died at West Miln in 1794, parents of Alexander, David, George, Patrick. [Rattray MI]

DUN, ALEXANDER, minister of Bendochy from 1747 to his death on 10 November 1784, husband of Elizabeth Ranken, parents of William, Anna, Elizabeth, and Alexander. [F.V.254]

DUNCAN, BARBARA, relict of John Pilmor in Kirkton of Rattray, a bond of corrobation, 1679. [NAS.RD3.45.28]

DUNCAN, PATRICK, an Elder of Alyth, 1671. [HA#108]

EASSON, JOHN, a gardener in Blairgowrie, indented with John McLeod a merchant in Edinburgh, to serve in Maryland or any other colony for five years, on 25 December 1741. [NAS.RH9.17/308]

EDWARD, GEORGE, a portioner in Coupar Angus, testament, 20 March 1736, Comm. Dunkeld. [NAS]

EDWARD, JOHN, in Alyth, 1653. [HA#96]

EDWARD, JOHN, a merchant in Coupar Angus, was admitted as a burgess of St Andrews on 25 August 1737. [St Andrews Burgh Court Book]

EDWARD, THOMAS, in Blairgowrie, a deed, 1707. [NAS.RD3.111/260]

EDWARD, WILLIAM, a merchant and brewer in Coupar Angus, deeds, 1682, 1705, 1714. [NAS.RD4.50.831; RD4.97.155; RD2.103.2.62; RD3.142.96]; testament, 24 September 1717, Comm. Dunkeld. [NAS]

EDWARD, WILLIAM, in Coupar Angus, testament, 9 March 1731, Comm. Dunkeld. [NAS]

ELDER, JOHN, born 1698, son of John Elder in Muirton of Ardblair, died 1722. [Blairgowrie MI]

ELLIOT, MARGARET, in Alyth, 1650. [HA#81]

FAIRWEATHER, THOMAS, in Alyth, 1650. [HA#81]

FARQUHAR, WILLIAM, a tailor from Alyth, a Jacobite in Ogilvy's Regiment, 1745-1746. [SHS.8.212]

FARQUHARSON, JAMES, in Coupar Angus, 1726. [NAS.GD68.1.300]

FELL, WILLIAM, a hammerman in Meigle, 1726. [NAS.GD68.1.300]

FENTON, DAVID, a mason in Alyth, 1667. [HA#103]

FERGUSON, HUGH, from Stanley, a Jacobite soldier of the Atholl Brigade, died in Perth on 15 April 1747. [P.1.186]

FIFE, JAMES, in Alyth, 1655. [HA#96]

FINDLAY, MARJORY, wife of John White a weaver in Coupar Angus, testament, 17 June 1756, Comm. Dunkeld. [NAS]

FINDLAY, THOMAS, a Deacon of Alyth parish, 1668. [HA#93]

FINLAW, ALEXANDER, born 1626, died 1662, husband of Agnes Blair, died 1679. [Meigle MI]

FINLAYSON, ALEXANDER, born 1692, minister of Eassie and Nevay from 1721 to his death on 12 September 1731, husband of ...... Finlayson, parents of Margaret. [F.V.260]

FISHER, DUNCAN, a merchant in Coupar Angus, deeds, 1705. [NAS.RD2.90/2.116/614; RD3.105.400]

FITHIE, WILLIAM, bailie of Alyth, 1649. [HA#81]

FITHIE, WILLIAM, in Balquhym, Alyth, a dissenter excommunicated in 1670. [HA#115]

FLEMING, DAVID, in Easter Bleaton, Rattray, testament, 29 June 1779, Comm. Dunkeld. [NAS]

FORBES, SAMUEL, a chapman in Alyth, testament, 1750, Comm. Dunkeld. [NAS]

FORMAN, JANET, found guilty of child-murder in Alyth, and transported to Perth in 1659. [HA#97]

FORRESTER, JAMES, notary in Alyth, 1603. [NAS.GD68.1.120]

FORRESTER, JOHN, in Alyth, a Deacon of Alyth parish, 1638. [HA#67]

FORRESTER, JOHN, in Pitnacrie of Alyth, a bond, 1671. [NAS.RD3.25.220]

FOULARTON, WILLIAM, died 1649, husband of Agnes, born 1632, died 1650. [Meigle MI]

FULLAR, BESSIE, born 1543, wife of Robert Doig in Bandoch, died 1610. [Meigle MI]

FULLARTON, WILLIAM, of that Ilk, 1675. [NAS.GD16.24.183]

FULLARTON, WILLIAM, in Meigle, a letter, 1745. [NAS.CH12.23.433]

FYFE, JAMES, tenant in Grange of Aberbothrie, Alyth, 1769. [NAS.GD83.I.381]

GEDDIE, JAMES, in Alyth, 1654. [HA#96]

GEEKIE, WILLIAM, of Parkhead, born 1695, died 1740, husband of Isabella Ogilvie, born 1708, died 1804. [Blairgowrie MI]

GEEKY, ELSPAT, born 1697, died 1750, wife of James Kyd in Chapelton. [Meigle MI]

GEIKIE, JOHN, a baker in Coupar Angus, testament, 31 July 1773, Comm. Dunkeld. [NAS]

GEILLOCH, GILBERT, a wright in Alyth, testament, 19 July 1758, Comm. Dunkeld. [NAS]

GIB, JOHN, in Alyth, 1650. [HA#81]

GLENNIE, PETER, a weaver in Pitnepy, Coupar Angus, a Jacobite soldier, 1745-1746. [SHS.8.214]

GORTIE, ALEXANDER, a wright in Alyth, 1663. [HA#102]

GORTIE, WILLIAM, in Alyth, 1665. [HA#97]

GOW, PETER, in Coupar Angus, testament, 1 June 1784, Comm. Dunkeld. [NAS]

GOWER, GEORGE, a workman from Alyth, a Jacobite in Ogilvy's Regiment, 1745-1746, transported to the colonies in 1747. [P.2.244]

GRAEME, ROBERT, in Meigle, a letter, 1745. [NAS.CH12.23.433]

GRAHAM, JOHN, minister of Meigle from 1687 to 1689. [F.V.270]

GRANT, JOHN, applied for an ale licence in Alyth, 1788. [NAS.B59.31.97]

GREIG, JAMES, a merchant in Coupar Angus, a deed, 1702. [NAS.RD4.90.252]

GREWER, JAMES, in Kirklands of Alyth, testament, 24 September 1741, Comm. Dunkeld. [NAS]

GUTHRIE, HENRY, minister of Bendochy from 1595 to 1633, and minister of Coupar Angus in 1611, husband of Elizabeth Small, parents of James, Henry, and Elizabeth. [F.V.253/258]

HACKNEY, DAVID, in Buchat, Alyth, testament, 9 August 1783, Comm. Dunkeld. [NAS]

HAGGART, DAVID, of Cairnmuir, Kirkhill, Caputh, a Jacobite sympathiser in 1745. [SHS.8.218]

HALL, THOMAS, a brewer in Alyth, testament, 18 March 1740, Comm. Dunkeld. [NAS]

HALLIBURTON, Dr GEORGE, minister at Coupar Angus from 1648 to 1682, [F.V.258]; bonds, 1675. [NAS.RD4.36.503; RD4.37.420]

HALYBURTON, ISABEL, born 1726, died July 1751, daughter of Patrick Halyburton in Muirton. [Alyth MI]

HAMILTON, JOHN, minister of Meigle from 1686 to 1689. [F.V.270]

HARDIE, WILLIAM, a parishioner of Coupar Angus, 1775. [NAS.CH2.395.6/6]

HAY, ALEXANDER, in Logie Meigle, testament, 5 December 1688, Comm. Dunkeld. [NAS]

HAY, GEORGE, minister of Coupar Angus from 1682 to 1698, husband of Margaret Hamilton, parents of William, George, James, Jean, Anna, and Margaret, [F.V.258]; a deed, 1700. [NAS.RD4.86.656]

HAY, JAMES, of Rattray, a tack, 1680. [NAS.RD4.47.486]

HAY, JAMES, a surgeon in Alyth, testament, 21 April 1761, Comm. Dunkeld. [NAS]

HAY, JAMES, a merchant in Coupar Angus, testament, 31 December 1774, Comm. Dunkeld. [NAS]

HENDERSON, ALEXANDER, an elder of Coupar Angus, 1775. [NAS.CH2.395.6/8]

HENDERSON, JAMES, born 1644, son of David Henderson in Hooptoun, died 20 May 1666. [Alyth MI]

HENDERSON, JAMES, in Little Balmile, Meigle, testament, 14 June 1712, Comm. Dunkeld. [NAS]

HENDERSON, JAMES, his wife Janet Anderson born 1707 died 1742, parents of Lawrance, Jamrs, William, Thomas and Yophens. [Rattray MI]

HENDERSON, JOHN, a merchant in Coupar Angus, deeds, 1705, 1706, 1707. [NAS.RD3.107.254, etc; RD2.91.59; RD3.113.203]

HENDERSON, LAURANCE, in Clayhills of Rattray, born 1659, died 1742. [Rattray MI]

HENDERSON, WILLIAM, in Alyth, 1665. [HA#97]

HENRYSON, WALTER, portioner of Bonniton of Rattray, 1644. [NAS.GD68.1.202]

HERON, JAMES, schoolmaster of Coupar Angus, a bond, 1683. [NAS.RD4.53.353]

HERRIES, JOHN, portioner of the Mains of Rattray, a bond of corrobation, 1680. [NAS.RD3.47.393]

HILL, DAVID, born 1737, a farmer in Tofthill, died 16 April 1812, husband of Janet Hunter, born 1733, died 9 May 1814. [Coupar Angus MI]

HILL, JAMES, in Blairgowrie, a letter, 1745. [NAS.CH12.23.451]

HOOD, JOHN, born 1633, a hammerman, died 1694, husband of Helen Slidders, born 1633, died 1694. [Meigle MI]

HUNTER, ALEXANDER, in Alyth, testament, 14 December 1738, Comm. Dunkeld. [NAS]

HUNTER, JAMES, in Jordanstone, a Deacon of Alyth parish, 1638. [HA#67]

HUNTER, JOHN, in Longlogie, Meigle, testament, 17 November 1758, Comm. Dunkeld. [NAS]

HUNTER, WILLIAM, a Deacon of Alyth parish, 1655. [HA#93]

HUTCHISON, JOHN, a drover in Coupar Angus, testament, 7 June 1800, Comm. Dunkeld. [NAS]

INSCHIACH, CHRISTIAN, an ale-seller in Alyth, 1650. [HA#81]

IRELAND, JAMES, in Balbrogoe, Coupar Angus, a bond, 1666. [NAS.RD4.16.484]

IRELAND, THOMAS, schoolmaster and Session Clerk of Alyth, 1653, bonds, 1675, 1678. [NAS.RD2.39.607; RD3.43.386][HA#94]

IRONS, ELIZABETH, in Myreside of Cannedy, Meigle, testament, 16 January 1690, Comm. Dunkeld. [NAS]

IRONS, JAMES, born 1659, died 1726. [Coupar Angus MI]

ISLES, THOMAS, in Meigle, husband of Janet Campbell born 1772, died 1799. [Meigle MI]

JAMIESON, DAVID, a merchant in Alyth, testament, 28 February 1751, Comm. Dunkeld. [NAS]

JAMIESON, WILLIAM, in Alyth, a deed, 1702. [NAS.RD4.90.582]

JOHNSTON, JAMES, born 1759, minister of Blairgowrie from 1787 to 1836, husband of (1) Jean Craigie, parents of Thomas, Jane, James, (2) Margaret Imlach or Anderson, died 12 October 1836. [F.V.256]

JOHNSTON, JOHN, in Alyth, a deed, 1702. [NAS.RD4.90.582]

JOHNSTON, JOHN, born 1749, a cooper in Coupar Angus, emigrated to Philadelphia in 1774. [NA.T47.12]

KAY, WILLIAM, in Meigle, testament, 14 December 1710, Comm. Dunkeld. [NAS]

KEA, JOHN, born 1642, farmer in Moss-side of Fullarton, died 1697, husband of Barbara Piper. [Meigle MI]

KEA, JOHN, born 1640, died 1705, husband of Jane Mustard, born 1655, died 1705, parents of John and William. [Meigle MI]

KEA, WILLIAM, born 1641, died 1704, husband of Janet Hay in Mains of Fullarton. [Meigle MI]

KEA, WILLIAM, born 1605, died 1635, husband of Isobel Taylor in Mains of Meigle. [Meigle MI]

KEAY, CHARLES, born 10 February 1740, second son of James Keay of Snaigow, minister of Coupar Angus from 1779 to his death on 9 April 1807. [F.V.258]

KER, JAMES, died 1649. [Alyth MI]

KID, JANET, born 1769, died 1 April 1806, wife of Charles Hendry miller at Quiech. [Alyth MI]

LAIRD, ALEXANDER, in Meigle, and his relict Jean Laird, testaments, 9 October 1716, 2 May 1717, and 9 November 1717, Comm. Dunkeld. [NAS]

LAIRD, ANDREW, born 1665, son of James Laird, died 1689. [Meigle MI]

LAIRD, JAMES, of Bendoch, born 1666, died 1723, husband of Jane Mitchell. [Meigle MI]

LAIRD, JOHN, born 1608, miller at the New Mill of Eassie, died 1657, husband of Jean Mill. [Meigle MI]

LAM, JOHN, in Alyth, 1666. [HA#96]

LAMMIE, SYLVESTER, son of Sylvester Lammie the minister of Glamis, minister of Eassie and Nevay from 1665 to 1701, dead by 1713, husband of Margaret Melvill, parents of John, Sylvester, and Helen. [F.V.260]

LAWSON, DAVID, a servant from Alyth, a Jacobite in Ogilvie's Regiment, 1745, fought at the Battle of Falkirk. [SHS.8.22]

LAWSON, THOMAS, a chapman from Alyth, a Jacobite in Ogilvie's Regiment 1745-1746. [P.2.234; SHS.8.222]

LEITCH, DAVID, minister of Coupar Angus in 1622. [F.V.258]

LINDSAY, ROBERT, born about 1591, schoolmaster then minister at Coupar Angus from 1625 to 1645, killed when the town was burned by Alister McDonald alias Colkitto, in April 1645 relict Margaret Rind, a bond, 1673. [NAS.RD4.34.343][F.V.258]

LINDSAY, THOMAS, a brewer in Alyth, testament, 15 August 1778, Comm. Dunkeld. [NAS]

LINDSAY, WILLIAM, minister of Meigle from 1677 to 1679. [F.V.270]

LISTER, ADAM, a vintner in Coupar Angus, testaments, 3 February and 2 June 1789, Comm. Dunkeld. [NAS]

LOUSON, JOHN, son of James Louson a baker in Dundee, minister of Alyth from 1686 to 1689, died on 20 May 1698. [F.V.250]

LOUSON, RONALD, in Kirkton of Rattray, a bond, 1672. [NAS.RD3.28.353]

LOUSON, THOMAS, portioner of the Mains of Rattray, bonds, 1674, 1679. [NAS.RD4.36.169; RD3.45.33]

LOW, ABRAHAM, in Coupar Grange, testament, 16 February 1688, Comm. Dunkeld. [NAS]

LOW, JAMES, a smith in Coupar Grange, testament, 4 July 1688, Comm. Dunkeld. [NAS]

LOW, JOHN, a hammerman in Alyth, testament, 16 May 1760, Comm. Dunkeld. [NAS]

LOW, JOHN, a hammerman and feuar in Alyth, younger son of Abraham Low, testament, 12 November 1776, Comm. Dunkeld. [NAS]

LUNDIE, THOMAS, born 1574, minister of Alyth from 1602 until his death on 8 June 1636, and his wife Jean Blair, born 1603, died 26 May 1636, parents of Grizel, Isobel, Magdalen, Jean, James, Robert, and Thomas. [Alyth MI][F.V.249]; a bond, 1632. [NAS.GD16.1.44/45]

LUNDIE, THOMAS, in Perth, sometime minister at Rattray, deeds, 1669. [NAS.RD4.24.546; RD2.25.778; RD3.21.50/61/112]

LYON, ANNA, relict of George Campbell in Coupar Angus, testament, 22 May 1727, Comm. Dunkeld. [NAS]

LYON, JAMES, born 1694, son of George Lyon of Wester Ogil and his wife Jean Nisbet, minister of Blairgowrie from 1722 to 1768, husband of Alison Gillespie, parents of George, Gabriel, Katherine, Robert, and Barbara, died 22 December 1768. [F.V.256]

MCCOMIE, ANDREW, a messenger in Coupar Angus, a deed, 1701. [NAS.RD4.89.65]

MCCREATH, WILLIAM, in Coupar Grange, testament, 1695, Comm. Dunkeld. [NAS]

MCDOUGALL, JAMES, a weaver in Alyth, was appointed as a constable in 1787. [NAS.B59.31.85]

MCKAY, JAMES, a surgeon in Blairgowrie, deceased, son of John McKay in Cairns, 1799. [NAS.GD16.38.6]

MACKIE, THOMAS, a Deacon of Alyth parish, 1658. [HA#93]

MACPHERSON, Colonel ALLAN, of Blairgowrie, father of William McPherson, 1776-1789, 1792. [NAS.GD80.900; CS228/B8/21]

MAIR, ELSPETH, relict of John Bruce, in Blacklunans, Alyth, testament, 1 January 1690, Comm. Dunkeld. [NAS]

MALCOLM, HARRY, born 1633, son of Robert Malcolm minister of Bendochy, minister of Bendochy from 1663 to his death in 1688, husband of Helen Small, parents of Robert and Henry. [F.V.253]

MALCOLM, HARRY, in Kinloch, Coupar Angus, testaments, 28 October 1714 and 10 July 1717, Comm. Dunkeld. [NAS]

MALCOLM, JAMES, in Aughter, Alyth, heir to his brother William Malcolm, 1714; a bond, 1715; a disposition, 1715. [NAS.GD16.3.188; GD1.931.32; GD83.I.470/1055]

MALCOLM, ROBERT, born about 1600, son of William Malcolm minister of Airlie, minister of Bendochy from 1631 to his death on 30 June 1663, husband of Margaret Guthrie, parents of Harry, William, Isobel and Elspeth. [F.V.253]

MALCOLM, WILLIAM, minister at Meigle from 1672 to 1678. [F.V.270] [NAS.GD254.667/668]

MALICE, MARGARET, born 1670, died 31 December 1703, wife of George Wighton a merchant. [Coupar Angus MI]

MALLIE, MARGARET, wife of George Robertson a merchant in Coupar Angus, a deed, 1707. [NAS.RD3.111.239]

MARSHALL, WILLIAM, tenant in Burnside, Alyth, testament, 29 May 1777, Comm. Dunkeld. [NAS]

MARSHALL, ALEXANDER, a merchant in Coupar Angus, testament, 27 April 1740, Comm. Dunkeld. [NAS]

MARTIN, CHRISTIAN, in Bogside of Coupar, relict of James Watson a flesher in Coupar Angus, testament, 23 November 1758, Comm. Dunkeld. [NAS]

MARTIN, JAMES, in Kirkton of Rattray, deed, 1672. [NAS. RD3.28.353]

MARTIN, JOHN, in Kirkton of Rattray, a bond, 1669. [NAS.RD4.23.820]

MATHERS, ELIZABETH, a deed, 1700. [NAS.RD4.87.432]

MATHERS, JOHN, minister of Alyth in 1690. [F.V.250]

MAXWELL, DAVID, minister of Eassie and Nevay from 1733 to 1751. [F.V.260]

MELISS, DAVID, a flesher in Coupar Angus, testament, 20 April 1773, Comm. Dunkeld. [NAS]

MENZIES, ISOBEL, in Coupar Angus, testament, 31 May 1777, Comm. Dunkeld. [NAS]

MENZIES, WILLIAM, a merchant in Coupar Angus, a deed, 1705. [NAS.RD3.107.266]

MILL, MARGARET, born 1623, died 1681. [Meigle MI]

MILL, MARGARET, in Bruchtie, Alyth, testament, 5 April 1690, Comm. Dunkeld. [NAS]

MILLER, JAMES, in Alyth, a deed, 1687. [NAS.RD2.68.1087]

MILLER, JAMES, born 1667, a wright in Coupar Angus, died 7 July 1735, husband of Isabel Playfair. [Alyth MI]; testament, 25 October 1743, Comm. Dunkeld. [NAS]

MILLER, THOMAS, a writer in Alyth, testament, 3 November 1738, Comm. Dunkeld. [NAS]

MILLER, THOMAS, born 1696, died 1755. [Meigle MI]

MILLER, WILLIAM, minister of Meigle from 1702 to 1708. [F.V.270]

MILN, JOHN, in Meigle, testament, 21 March 1726, Comm. Dunkeld. [NAS]

MILNE, WILLIAM, and his daughter Elspeth, in Logie Meigle, testament, 16 April 1741, Comm. Dunkeld. [NAS]

MITCHELL, JAMES, an elder of Coupar Angus, 1775. [NAS.CH2.395.6/8]

MITCHELL, MARGARET, in Causewayend, Coupar Angus, widow of Andrew Donn a flesher there, testament, 19 June 1766, Comm. Dunkeld. [NAS]

MITCHELL, PHILIP, in Rattray, testament, 29 July 1766, Comm. Dunkeld. [NAS]

MITCHELL, THOMAS, minister of Coupar Angus from 1699 to 1702. [F.V. 258]

MITCHELL, WILLIAM, in Logie Meigle, testament, 7 April 1690, Comm. Dunkeld. [NAS]

MONCREIFF, MALCOLM, a merchant in Coupar Angus, deeds, 1686, 1697. [NAS.RD3.64.275; RD2.80/2.585]

MONCREIFF, WILLIAM, a litster in Alyth, 1666; deeds, 1685, 1686; testament, 5 July 1688, Comm. Dunkeld. [HA#96][NAS.RD4.56.736; RD4.59.502]

MONCUR, DAVID, a brewer in Alyth, testament, 17 June 1720, Comm. Dunkeld. [NAS]

MONCUR, JAMES, son of John Moncur in Bonniton of Rattray, a bond, 1676. [NAS.RD4.39.95]

MONIEDATH, WILLIAM, in Cupar Grange, testament, 14 May 1695, Comm. Dunkeld. [NAS]

MORISON, DANIEL, in Kirkton of Rattray, testament, 1695, Comm. Dunkeld. [NAS]

MORRISON, DONALD, portioner of the Milton of Rattray, a bond, 1674. [NAS.RD4.36.171]

MORRISON, GEORGE, a writer in the Kirkton of Rattray, 1603. [NAS.GD68.1.120]

MUNRO, HENRY, in Alyth, 1667. [HA#97]

MUNRO, MARY, born 1708, died 1734, wife of Alexander Robertson. [Alyth MI]

MURDOCH, JOHN, a merchant in Alyth, a bond, 1682. [NAS.RD4.51.288]

MURRAY, JAMES, a tailor in Coupar Angus, testament, 12 December 1717, Comm. Dunkeld. [NAS]

MUSTARD, ALEXANDER, a merchant in Alyth, a deed, 1688; testament, 14 June 1688, Comm. Dunkeld. [NAS.RD3.68.308]

MUSTARD, DAVID, son of William Mustard in Kirkton of Rattray, a bond, 1673. [NAS.RD4.33.494]

MUSTARD, JAMES, a tenant in Grange, testament, 25 May 1762, Comm. Dunkeld. [NAS]

MUSTARD, JEAN, relict of William Murray in Meigle, testament, 28 February 1751, Comm. Dunkeld. [NAS]

MUSTARD, JOHN, in Alyth, testament, 28 January 1748, Comm. Dunkeld. [NAS]

MUSTARD, KATHLEEN, died 1737, wife of James Rattray miller at Nether Loggie. [Meigle MI]

MYLES, DAVID, a baxter in Coupar Angus, testament, 19 January 1731, Comm. Dunkeld. [NAS]

NAIRNE, WILLIAM, of Kirkhill, 1675. [NAS.GD16.24.183]

NAIRNE, WILLIAM, in Meigle, a letter, 1745. [NAS.CH12.23.433]

NAPIER, JOHN, born 1643, died 1674, in Mains of Meigle, husband of Janet Hay. [Meigle MI]

NICOLSON, JOHN, minister of Meigle from 1661 to 1666. [F.V.270]

NIVEN, DAVID, a feuar in Alyth, and his spouse Isobel Mitchell, testament, 29 July 1742, Comm. Dunkeld. [NAS]

NIVEN, JAMES, a brewer in Alyth, testament, 2 February 1748, Comm. Dunkeld. [NAS]

NIVEN, JOHN, a Deacon of Alyth parish, 1653. [HA#93]

OGILVIE, ANDREW, in Coupar Grange, testament, 9 April 1690, Comm. Dunkeld. [NAS]

OGILVIE, JAMES, of the barony of Cluny, Meigle, 1672, 1675. [NAS.GD16.5.75; GD16.24.183]

OGILVIE, JAMES, bailie depute of the Regality of Cupar, testaments, 19 October 1714, 18 August 1715, and 29 October 1717, Comm. Dunkeld. [NAS]

OGILVIE, JAMES, in Coupar Grange, testaments, 7 November 1732 and 7 June 1735, Comm. Dunkeld. [NAS]

OGILVY, JAMES, born 1727, son of George Ogilvy minister of Kirriemuir, minister of Eassie and Nevay from 1752 to his death on 20 June 1802, husband of Susan Ogilvie, parents of George, Anna, David, William, and James. [F.V.260]

OGILVIE, JOHN, of Whiteside, an Elder of Alyth parish, 1658. [HA#93]

OGILVIE, JOHN, and wife Isobel Ogilvie, in Inchioch, Alyth, 1669; dissenters excommunicated in 1670. [HA#100/115]

OGILVIE, JOHN, in Burnside of Alyth, bonds, 1677, 1679, 1682, 1683. [NAS.RD2.44.565; RD4.45.534; RD3.51.332; RD4.53.111]

OGILVIE, JOHN, late bailie of Coupar Angus, testaments, 31 January 1728 and 16 October 1735, Comm. Dunkeld. [NAS]

OGILVIE, JOHN, only son of the late John Ogilvie late bailie depute of the Regality of Coupar Angus, testament, 13 January 1736, Comm. Dunkeld. [NAS]

OGILVIE, MARGARET, relict of Alexander Airth schoolmaster of Coupar Angus, testaments, 4 May and 16 November 1749, Comm. Dunkeld. [NAS]

OGILVIE, THOMAS, of Turfechie, bailie of the town and barony of Alyth, 1684. [HA#117]

OGILVIE, THOMAS, eldest son of Thomas Ogilvie of Turfaudry, minister of Coupar Angus from 1703 to his death on 22 May 1741, husband of Elizabeth Smith, parents of Henry, Elizabeth, and Isobel. [F.V.258]

OGILVIE, THOMAS, a brewer in Alyth, testament, 29 December 1731, Comm. Dunkeld. [NAS]

OLIPHANT, GEORGE, of Clasbenie, Errol, and Helen Ramsay, daughter of Sir James Ramsay of Bamf, marriage contract, 1697. [NAS.GD83.I. 562]

OLIPHANT, JAMES, a litster in Alyth, husband of Anna Herring, a bond, 1676. [NAS.RD4.39.468]

OLIPHER, JOHN, in Bermanie, Alyth, testament, 4 July 1688, Comm. Dunkeld. [NAS]

OWLER, WILLIAM, tenant of pendicles in the parish of Blairgowrie, a tack, 1794. [NAS.GD83.746]

PATERSON, DONALD, in Auchterhouse, parish of Coupar Angus, testament, 22 June 1775, Comm. Dunkeld. [NAS]

PATON, THOMAS, alias Neil Stewart, in Coupar Angus, testament, 7 March 1745, Comm. Dunkeld. [NAS]

PATTILLO, JOHN, a bailie and an Elder of Alyth parish, 1661. [HA#93]

PAUL, MAGDALEN, born 1708, died 1764, wife of John Baxter a weaver in Longley. [Meigle MI]

PETRIE, GEORGE, an elder of Coupar Angus, 1775. [NAS.CH2.395.6/8]

PHILIP, JAMES, a brewer in Alyth, testament, 21 May 1779, Comm. Dunkeld. [NAS]

PILMOR, ALEXANDER, sheriff clerk of Coupar Angus, a deed, 1685. [NAS.RD2.65.507]

PILMOR, JAMES, a notary in Coupar Angus, husband of Elizabeth Ramsay, a bond, 1674. [NAS.RD4.35.760]

PILMOR, JEAN, daughter of the late James Pilmor, a merchant in Blairgowrie, and his wife Isobel Wilson, a pre-nuptial contract, 1764. [NAS.GD83/568]

PILMOR, JOHN, a tailor in Kirkton of Rattray, bond/tack, 1674, 1675, 1677. [NAS.RD4.35.453; RD3.38.88; RD4.40.701; RD3.43.39]

PILMOR, JOHN, a brewer in Coupar Angus, a deed, 1700. [NAS.RD4.87.294]

PILMOR, JOHN, and his spouse Isabel Murray in Alyth, testament, 14 March 1750, Comm. Dunkeld. [NAS]

PILMOR, WILLIAM, in Halton of Rattray, testament, 4 July 1690, Comm. Dunkeld. [NAS]

PLAYFAIR, Dr JAMES, born 1752 son of Charles Playfair and his wife Catherine Henderson, minister at Meigle from 1777 to 1800, minister of Bendochy from 1785 to his death on 22 April 1812, husband of Grizel Duncan, parents of Katherine, Patrick, Charles, James, George, and David. [F.V.254/271]; a letter,1799. [NAS.GD1.1009.23]

PORTER, DAVID, born 1658, died 1718, husband of Agnes Stinson, born 1662, died 1733, in Myreside of Fullarton. [Meigle MI]

PRINGLE, ROBERT, son of James Pringle an apothecary in Coupar Angus, and his factor, a deed, 1696. [NAS.RD4.79.328]

PULLAR, JOHN, in Little Barrie, Alyth, testament, 4 April 1690, Comm. Dunkeld. [NAS]

PURGAVIE, GEORGE, in Hillhead of Rattray, a bond, 1677. [NAS.RD4.40.602]

RAMSAY, ALEXANDER, in Alyth, a cautioner, 1632; an Elder of Alyth parish, 1638. [HA#67][NAS.GD16.1.44]

RAMSAY, BEATRIX, in Alyth, testament, 23 March 1773, Comm. Dunkeld. [NAS]

RAMSAY, DAVID, of Balharrie, an Elder of Alyth, 1671. [HA#108]

RAMSAY, DAVID, of Jordonstoun, an Elder of Alyth parish, 1658. [HA#93]

RAMSAY, DAVID, son of John Ramsay, portioner of Milton of Rattray, bonds, 1674, 1675. [NAS.RD4.35.775/776; RD4.37.407]

RAMSAY, DAVID, in Milton of Rattray, a bond of corrobation, 1677. [NAS.RD3.43.37]

RAMSAY, ELIZABETH, widow of John Ogilvy a vintner in Coupar Angus, testament, 4 December 1782, Comm. Dunkeld. [NAS]

RAMSAY, GILBERT, feuar of Bamff, an Elder of Alyth parish, 1638. [HA#67]

RAMSAY, Sir GILBERT, of Bamff, Elder of Alyth, 1671. [HA#108]

RAMSAY, GILBERT, son and heir of Gilbert Ramsay of Tilliemurdoch, Alyth, 1715. [NAS.GD83.I.349]

RAMSAY, GILBERT, a surgeon in Coupar Angus, son of James Ramsay of Tilliemurdon, a pre-nuptial contract, 1764. [NAS.GD83.568]

RAMSAY, JAMES, schoolmaster and Session Clerk of Alyth, 1658-1661. [HA#94]

RAMSAY, JAMES, in Whiteside of Alyth, a bond, 1673. [NAS.RD4.32.521]

RAMSAY, JAMES, portioner of Milton of Rattray, a deed, 1690. [NAS.RD3.73.237]

RAMSAY, JAMES, of Parkconnar, minister of Bendochy from 1700 to his death on 16 August 1746, husband of (1) Margaret Lyon, (2) Barbara Murray, parents of Christian. [F.V.254]

RAMSAY, JANET, in Rattray, testament, 14 December 1769, Comm. Dunkeld. [NAS]

RAMSAY, JOHN, born around 1614, minister of Blairgowrie from 1649 to 1663, died in October 1663, husband of Helen Symmer, parents of Alexander, John, David and James. [F.V.255]

RAMSAY, JOHN, of Bastardbank, an Elder of Alyth parish, 1658. [HA#93]

RAMSAY, JOHN, of Milne of Quich, Elder of Alyth, 1671. [HA#108]

RAMSAY, JOHN, a writer in Alyth, testament, 6 January 1726, Comm. Dunkeld. [NAS]

RAMSAY, PATRICK, at the Milnetoun of Rattray, a deed, 1707. [NAS.RD2.93.448]

RAMSAY, THOMAS, schoolmaster and Session Clerk of Alyth, 1661. [HA#95]

RAMSAY, THOMAS, in Westmoreland, Cornwall, Jamaica, youngest brother of Sir George Ramsay of Banff, letter of attorney, 1790. [NAS.GD83.I.1065]

RAMSAY, WILLIAM, a bailie and Elder of Alyth, 1672, bonds, 1673, 1677, 1682; testament, 8 July 1700, Comm. Dunkeld. [NAS.RD4.32.521; RD4.40.602; RD2.57.227][HA#108]

RANKEN, DAVID, born 1663, son of Alexander Ranken of Pottie and his wife Agnes Reid, minister of Bendochy from 1692 to 1700, died 17 November 1728, husband of Euphan Blair. [F.V.253]

RATTRAY, ALEXANDER, son of David Rattray of Dalrylean, charter, 1683. [NAS.NRAS.2474.9]

RATTRAY, ALEXANDER, husband of Euphame Ogilvie, parents of Alexander, died 1736, Elizabeth, died 1736, Robert, died 1738, and Elizabeth, died 1742. [Meigle MI]

RATTRAY, CHARLES, son of William Rattray late minister of Cargill, a sasine, 1737. [NAS.GD170.140]

RATTRAY, DAVID, feuar of Ranagullan, 1680; an Elder of Alyth parish, 1638, 1656. [HA#67/94][NAS.GD83.I.840]

RATTRAY, DAVID, of West Forrest, an Elder of Alyth parish, 1658, 1671. [HA#93/108]

RATTRAY, JAMES, son of David Rattray of Rannagullon, 1680, Elder of Alyth, 1671. [HA#108]; charter of Kirkhilloch, Glen Isla, 1696. [NAS.NRAS.2474.10; GD83.I.840]

RATTRAY, JOHN, in Balquheam, an Elder of Alyth parish, 1638. [HA#67]

RATTRAY, JOHN, minister at Rattray and Alyth from 1629 to 1669, died 1678, bonds, 1673, 1679. [NAS.RD2.36.196; RD4.45.267]; husband of Margaret Ramsay, born 1606, died 24 May 1671, parents of John, Patrick, William, Margaret, Elizabeth, Isobel, Helen, and Jean. [F.V. 249]

RATTRAY, JOHN, of Mylnhall, 1670, 1675, husband of Margaret and father of Anne, 1677. [NAS.GD16.24.183/184; GD16.27.81]

RATTRAY, JOHN, of Boreland, Alyth, testament, 2 April 1705, Comm. Dunkeld. [NAS]

RATTRAY, JOHN, a merchant in Alyth, testament, 29 March 1722, Comm. Dunkeld. [NAS]

RATTRAY, PATRICK, in Wester Whyteside of Alyth, husband of Catherine Smith, parents of Elspet, a bond, 1679. [NAS.RD4.44.483]

RATTRAY, SILVESTER, in Broomhill, Alyth, testament, 9 October 1690, Comm. Dunkeld. [NAS]

RATTRAY, WALTER, in Blair, husband of Christian Valentine, a tack, 1672. [NAS.RD3.30.315]

RATTRAY, WILLIAM, in Borland, an Elder of Alyth in 1643, 1650. [HA#67/83]

RATTRAY, WILLIAM, from Alyth, a soldier of the army under the Duke of Hamilton that invaded England in support of King Charles I in 1648. [HA#85]

RATTRAY, WILLIAM, clerk to the Regality of Coupar Angus, testament, 22 January 1760, Comm. Dunkeld. [NAS]

REID, GEORGE, and his wife Margaret Burd in Muir of Kirkhill, parents of Elizabeth (1701-1726), Margaret, Jean, Ann, Thomas, William, and Gilbert. [Meigle MI]

REID, JANET, in Blacklunans, parish of Alyth, 1668. [HA#97]

REOCH, JOHN, a cooper from Stanley, Auchergaven, a Jacobite soldier, 1745-1746. [SHS.8.232]

ROBERTSON, ALEXANDER, son and heir of Leonard Robertson of Straloch, a precept of clare constat, 1717. [NAS.GD83.I.484]

ROBERTSON, CHARLES, a bailie in Coupar Angus, a deed, 1692. [NAS.RD4.70.218]

ROBERTSON, GEORGE, a merchant in Coupar Angus, husband of Margaret Malice, widow of George Wichtan of Boghall, deeds, 1702,1705, 1707, 1711,1714. [NAS.RD4.90.477; RD2.90/1.849; RD2.93.428, etc; RD4.115.873; GD83.I.593]

ROBERTSON, JAMES, the younger, a merchant in Coupar Angus, deeds, 1705, 1707. [NAS.RD2.90/2.677, etc; RD2.94.565, etc]

ROBERTSON, JOHN, an Elder of Alyth parish, 1650. [HA#83]

ROBERTSON, JOHN, of Tullymurdoch, Elder of Alyth, 1671. [HA#108]

ROBERTSON, JOHN, born 1713, a weaver, died 1745, husband of Agnes Butchart in Fullarton. [Meigle MI]

ROBERTSON, JOHN, born 1709, minister of Alyth from 1737 until his death on 3 June 1772, husband of Margaret Meek. [F.V.250]

ROBERTSON, ROBERT, in Bonnyton of Rattray, 1644. [NAS.GD68.1.202]

ROBERTSON, ROBERT, tenant in Nether Cloquhat, 1790. [NS.GD83.I. 738]

ROBERTSON, THOMAS, minister at Alyth from 1669 to his death in November 1685, husband of (1) Isobel Rattray, parents of John, Margaret, Thomas, and Isobel, (2) Anne Haliburton, parents of James, Margaret, Alexander, and Anna, [F.V.250]; a bond, 1680. [NAS.RD4.46.574][HA#107]

ROBERTSON, WILLIAM, husband of Janet Gordon (1699-1738) daughter of John Gordon in Balmackeron. [Meigle MI]

RODGER, GEORGE, in Rattray, testament, 10 April 1690, Comm. Dunkeld. [NAS]

RODGER, JAMES, in Blairgowrie, deeds, 1696. [NAS.RD4.79.1095/1096]

ROSS, JOHN, of Magdalens, minister of Blairgowrie 1603-1648,son of John Ross of Craigie, husband of Jean, Shaw, parents of John, [F.V, 255]; 1627. [NAS.GD190/2/118]

ROY, GEORGE, overseer and nursery gardener at the soldiers' settlement of Strelitz, letters, 1763-1768. [NAS.E777.120]

ROY, JANET, a vagabond in Alyth, 1648. [HA#81]

RUSSELL, WILLIAM, a gardener in Meigle, testament, 1 March 1737, Comm. Dunkeld. [NAS]

SALTER, AGNES, in Alyth, widow of a soldier killed at the Battle of Dunbar, 1651. [HA#90]

SALTER, AGNES, in Pitnacrie, widow of a soldier killed at the Battle of Dunbar, 1651. [HA#90]

SALTER, JAMES, in Alyth, 1665. [HA#97]

SALTER, PATRICK, the younger in Alyth, was admitted as a Deacon of Alyth parish in 1638. [HA#67]

SANDERS, JOHN, in Coupar Angus, a deed, 1688. [NAS.RD4.63.430]

SANDEMAN, AGNES, in Alyth, guilty of lewd practices, taken to the Perth Workhouse in 1741. [NAS.B59.31.27]

SANDEMAN, ALEXANDER, a smith in Alyth, husband of Jean Finlay, a bond, 1670. [NAS.RD2.27.136][HA#103]

SANDEMAN, ANDREW, a smith in Alyth, 1637. [HA#66]

SANDEMAN, JANET, relict of James Murray in Little Bamff, Alyth, testament, 13 April 1759, Comm. Dunkeld. [NAS]

SANDEMAN, WILLIAM, in Faulds of Bamff, Alyth, testament, 3 January 1785, Comm. Dunkeld. [NAS]

SANDERSON, ANDREW, born 1671, died 1734, his wife ......, born 1644, died 1718. [Blairgowrie MI]

SANDY, JAMES, born 1766, an artist and feuar in Alyth, died 3 April 1819. [Alyth MI]

SCOBIE, JEAN, brewer in Coupar Angus, testament, 8 June 1727, Comm. Dunkeld. [NAS]

SCOTT, ALEXANDER, minister at Meigle from 1757 to his death on 28 November 1776, husband of Euphemia Henderson, parents of Thomas and William, [F.V.271]; testaments, 8 January 1777 and 25 May 1781, Comm. Dunkeld. [NAS]

SCOTT, JAMES, son of David Scott in Meigle, 1726. [NAS.GD68.1.300]

SCRYMGEOUR, JOHN, an apothecary in Alyth, testaments, 10 March 1726, 1 July 1729, and 29 June 1731, Comm. Dunkeld. [NAS]

SIM, ANTHONY, born 1727, died 4 February 1794, husband of Agnes Grant, born 1715, died 20 March 1799. [Coupar Angus MI]

SIMPSON, ANDREW, born in Coupar Angus before 1656, son of James Simpson and his wife Barbara Young, emigrated to Memel in 1678, a merchant there, died in January 1688. [SG.27.4.130]

SIMPSON, JOHN, a merchant in Cupar, a deed, 1686. [NAS.RD4.58.416]

SIMPSON, MARGARET, a parishioner of Coupar Angus, 1775. [NAS.CH2.395.6/6]

SIMPSON, PATRICK, a parishioner of Alyth, 1651. [HA#95]

SMALL, JEAN, born 1679, wife of John Irven, died 1743. [Blairgowrie MI]

SMALL, JOHN, and his spouse Elspeth McGibbon, in the Mains of Rattray, testament, 30 July 1691, Comm. Dunkeld. [NAS]

SMALL, ROBERT, an elder of Coupar Angus, 1775. [NAS.CH2.395.6/8]

SMALL, THOMAS, born 1744, minister of the Associate congregation in Coupar Angus, died 2 May 1772. [Coupar Angus MI]

SMALL, WILLIAM, an elder of Coupar Angus, 1775. [NAS.CH2.395.6/8]

SMALL, WILLIAM, tenant in Culdham, Coupar Angus, testament, 30 May 1782, Comm. Dunkeld. [NAS]

SMITH, ALEXANDER, in Alyth, a bond, 1680; testament, 29 July 1714, Comm. Dunkeld. [NAS.RD4.48.324]

SMITH, DAVID, beadle of Alyth, 1661. [HA#101]

SMITH, ISOBEL, spouse to James Turnbull, in Auchter Alyth, Alyth, testament, 4 July 1688, Comm. Dunkeld. [NAS]

SMITH, JAMES, in Kirkton of Rattray, testament, 9 April 1690, Comm. Dunkeld. [NAS]

SMITH, JOHN, was appointed schoolmaster at Meigle in 1692, testaments, 2 October 1728, 6 November 1733, and 8 July 1736, Comm. Dunkeld. [NAS.E53.30; E221.7.2]

SMITH, KATHERINE, spouse to Walter Rattray a webster in Little Blair, Blairgowrie, testament, 1598, Comm. St Andrews. [NAS]

SMYTON, GEORGE, an elder of Coupar Angus, 1775. [NAS.CH2.395.6/8]

SMYTON, GEORGE, son of George Smyton a baker in Coupar Angus, 1775. [NAS.CH2.395.6/8]

SOUTAR, ABRAHAM, an alleged sheepstealer in Alyth, 1650. [HA#81]

SOUTAR, ALEXANDER, a merchant in Alyth, a deed, 1672. [NAS.RD3.31.244]

SOUTAR, GEORGE, a merchant in Blairgowrie, testament, 1780, Comm. St Andrews. [NAS]

SOUTAR, JAMES, in Alyth, 1653; Elder of Alyth, 1671. [HA#95/108]

SOUTAR, JAMES, in Blair, relict Catherine Sanders, a deed, 1672. [NAS.RD3.30.315]

SOUTAR, JAMES, portioner of Coupar Grange, and his relict Margaret Husband, testament, 16 June 1688, Comm. Dunkeld. [NAS]

SOUTAR, JEAN, spouse to Thomas Makie, in Over Moorton, Alyth, testaments, 10 December 1686 and 14 July 1688, Comm. Dunkeld. [NAS]

SOUTAR, MARGARET, a parishioner of Coupar Angus, 1775. [NAS.CH2.395.6/8]

SOUTAR, THOMAS, son of Thomas Soutar in Alyth, a merchant burgess in Lowicz, Poland, 1637. [RGSS.IX.659]

SOUTAR, THOMAS, a merchant in Blairgowrie, heir to his father James Soutar a portioner there, 1759. [NAS.S/H]; a vintner and brewer in Blairgowrie, testament, 1778, Comm. St Andrews. [NAS]

SOUTAR, THOMAS, tenant of Wellton of Creuches, parish of Blairgowrie, a tack, 1791. [NAS.GD83.743]

SOUTAR, WILLIAM, a Deacon of Alyth parish, 1638. [HA#67]

SPALDING, ANDREW, of Ashintullie, a charter, 1683. [NAS.NRAS.2474.9]

SPALDING, ANDREW, in Myreside of Kirkhill, Meigle, testaments, 1652/1653, Comm. Dunblane. [NAS]

SPALDING, GEORGE, in Blair, testament, 1591, Comm. St Andrews. [NAS]

SPALDING, JANET, spouse to William Dick in Lochend of Blair, testament, 1591, Comm. St Andrews. [NAS]

SPALDING, ROBERT, an Elder of Alyth parish, 1650. [HA#83]

SPALDING, WILLIAM, an Elder of Alyth parish in 1643. [HA#67]

SPALDING, WILLIAM, in Thriethorns of Gormak, Blairgowrie, testament, 1615, Comm. St Andrews. [NAS]

SPALDING, WILLIAM, in Blacklunans, an Elder of Alyth parish, 1638. [HA#67]

SPANKIE, JAMES or THOMAS, born 1711, minister at Coupar Angus from 1742 his death on 3 May 1778, husband of Margaret Inglis, parents of Rachel, Thomas, Ann, George, Isobel, and Margaret, [F.V.258]; testaments, 15 March and 12 June 1779, Comm. Dunkeld. [NAS]

SPENCE, ADAM, born 1754, a feuar in Alyth, died 10 September 1818, husband of Jean Stewart. [Alyth MI]

SPENCE, JOHN, the elder, in Middlemyre, Blairgowrie, testament, 14 April 1618, Comm. St Andrews. [NAS]

SPROUL, JOHN, a drover in Coupar Angus, a deed, 1714. [NAS.RD2.104.43]

STEILL, ALEXANDER, and his wife Janet Adam, died by 1717. [Alyth MI]

STEILL, JAMES, in Westquarter, Alyth, and his youngest son James, a bond, 1629. [NAS.GD16.1.37]

STEILL, JOHN, the younger, and his wife Margaret Adam, in Westquarter, Alyth, a bond, 1629. [NAS.GD16.1.37]

STEILL, JOHN, in Leitvie, an Elder of Alyth, 1672. [HA#108]

STEILL, PATRICK, at 'ye bot of Bermenie', a Deacon of Alyth parish, 1638. [HA#67]

STEPHEN, MARJORY, in Fullerton, Meigle, testament, 18 January 1759, Comm. Dunkeld. [NAS]

STEVENSON, JOHN, in Meigle, testament, 4 September 1712, Comm. Dunkeld. [NAS]

STEWART, ALEXANDER, factor to James Hay of Rattray, a tack, 1680. [NAS.RD4.47.486]

STEWART, Major JAMES, of Bachrie, Blairgowrie, testament, 1688, Comm. St Andrews. [NAS]

STEWART, WALTER, of Easter Caputh, residing at Banchry milne, Blairgowrie, testament, 1717, Comm. St Andrews. [NAS]

STEWART, WILLIAM, minister of Blairgowrie from 1702 to 1721. [F.V. 256]

STINSON, WILLIAM, born 1676, died 1694, son of Robert Stinson and Elizabeth Kae in Myreside of Fullarton. [Meigle MI]

SYME, JOHN, in Hilton of Mains, Blairgowrie, testament, 1626, Comm. St Andrews. [NAS]

SYME, JOHN, a merchant in Coupar Angus, a bond, 1676. [NAS.RD4.39.459]

SYMERS, COLIN, son of Colin Symers a cordiner in Dundee, minister of Alyth from 1773 until his death on 22 January 1817, husband of Helen Hallyburton, parents of David, Margaret, Elizabeth, Colin, Helen, Amelia, Euphemia, Mary, John, Janet, James, Lilias, John, Thomas, and George, [F.V.251]; a bond, 1789. [NAS.GD16.3.206]

SYMMER, GEORGE, minister of Eassie and Nevay from 1603 to 1615; minister of Meigle from 1622 to ...., died 13 February 1655, husband of Margaret Fullarton, patents of John, Alexander, etc. [F.V.259/270]

SYMMER, JOHN, born 1607, minister of Meigle from 1634 to his death on 9 July 1660, husband of Margaret Campbell, parents of Alexander and Helen. [F.V.270]

THOM, DAVID, in West Drummie, Alyth, testament, 18 December 1782, Comm. Dunkeld. [NAS]

THOMSON, ADAM, in Alyth, 1653. [HA#95]

THOMSON, DAVID, portioner of Kingskettle, minister of Meigle from 1710 to his death on 24 April 1757, husband of Helen Myles, parents of David, Margaret, and James. [F.V.270]

THOMSON, JOHN, minister of Alyth from 1702 until his death on 29 December 1719, father of Jean. [F.V.250]

THOMSON, WALTER, in Little Blair, testament, 1624, Comm. St Andrews. [NAS]

TULLOCH, MARGARET, spouse of John Ogilvie, bailie depute of Coupar Angus, deed, 1714. [NAS.RD4.115.419]

TURNBULL, JEAN, spouse of James Sym in Coupar Angus, testament, 8 April 1689, Comm. Dunkeld. [NAS]

TURNBULL, JOHN, in Knockinaker, Blairgowrie, testament, 1685, Comm. St Andrews. [NAS]

TYRIE, WILLIAM, born 1678, died 1746, husband of Janet Findlay. [Meigle MI]

WALLACE, WILLIAM, a wright in Bonnyton of Rattray, 1644. [NAS.GD68.1.202]

WARDEN, JAMES, a schoolmaster in Alyth, 1750. [NAS.E736/6]

WATSON, THOMAS, a maltman in Chapelton, husband of Grizel Christie who died 1726. [Meigle MI]

WATSON, WILLIAM, born 1694, died 1761. [Meigle MI]

WEBSTER, DAVID, late schoolmaster in Arbroath, was appointed schoolmaster in Coupar Angus in 1775. [NAS.CH2.395.6/12]

WEST, JANET, a baker in Coupar Angus, testament, 5 April 1800, Comm. Dunkeld. [NAS]

WHITEHEAD, Mr, in Alyth, 1733. [NAS.B59.28.94]

WHITSON, PATRICK, in Luftie, Alyth, testament, 28 October 1711, Comm. Dunkeld. [NAS]

WHITSON, PATRICK, a writer in Coupar Angus, was admitted as a burgess of St Andrews on 15 November 1738. [St Andrews Burgh Court Book]

WHITSON, THOMAS, a notary in Rattray, a bond, 1679. [NAS.RD4.46.125]

WIDDER, ROBERT, a Deacon of Alyth parish, 1653. [HA#93]

WIGHT, JOHN, in Halton of Rattray, testament, 18 August 1747, Comm. Dunkeld. [NAS]

WIGHTON, GEORGE, of Boghall, husband of Margaret Malice, a disposition, 1703. [NAS.GD83.1.558]

WIGHTON, GEORGE, a merchant in Coupar Angus, testament, 28 March 1710, Comm. Dunkeld. [NAS]

WIGHTON, GEORGE, a merchant in Coupar Angus, and his daughter Agnes, testament, 9 August 1733, Comm. Dunkeld. [NAS]

WIGHTON, JAMES, a merchant in Coupar Angus, a bond, 5 April 1690; testament, 21 January 1702, Comm. Dunkeld. [NAS.GD83.I.576]

WIGHTON, JOHN, in Alyth, 1650. [HA#83]

WILKIE, DAVID, in Coupar Angus, bonds, 1680. [NAS.RD4.47.411/612]

WILSON, DAVID, born 1707, died 1763, father of James Wilson in Haughhead of Bandoch. [Alyth MI]

WILSON, HUGH, a merchant in Alyth, testament, 18 June 1718, Comm. Dunkeld. [NAS]

WILSON, JOHN, in Mawes, Blairgowrie, testament, 1635, Comm. St Andrews. [NAS]

WILSON, JOHN, merchant in Coupar Angus, testaments, 6 September 1770 and 1 February 1773 , Comm. Dunkeld. [NAS]

WILSON, MARGARET, born 1674, died 1698, wife of James Jack in Blair. [Blairgowrie MI]

WILSON, SILVESTER, in Fullarton, Meigle, testament, 10 December 1778, Comm. Dunkeld. [NAS]

WILSON, THOMAS, schoolmaster and Session Clerk in Alyth, 1656-1658. [HA#94]

WINDRAM, WILLIAM, a dyer at the Waulk-Milne of Coupar Angus, testament, 11 December 1739 and 16 December 1740, Comm. Dunkeld. [NAS]

WRIGHT, JOHN, in Halton of Rattray, testament, 2 December 1746, Comm. Dunkeld. [NAS]

YEAMAN, DAVID, at the Easter Waulkmill of Rattray, born 1600, died 1661. [Rattray MI]

YEAMAN, JAMES, at the West Waulkmilne of Rattray, testament, 8 September 1768, Comm. Dunkeld. [NAS]

YEAMAN, PATRICK, in the Kirkton of Rattray, a bond, 1672. [NAS.RD3.28.353]

YOUNG, GEORGE, merchant in Coupar Angus, testament, 16 May 1772, Comm. Dunkeld. [NAS]

REFERENCES

AJ = Aberdeen Journal, series

EEC = Edinburgh Evening Courant, series

GM = Gentleman's Magazine, series

HA = History of Alyth Parish Church, J. Meikle, [Edinburgh, 1933]

MI = Monumental Inscription

NA = National Archives, London

NAS = National Archives of Scotland, Edinburgh

P   = Prisoners of the '45, B. Seton, [Edinburgh, 1929]

RGSS = Register of the Great Seal of Scotland

SG = The Scottish Genealogist, series

SHS = Scottish History Society

www.ingramcontent.com/pod-product-compliance
Lightning Source LLC
Chambersburg PA
CBHW070927270326
41927CB00011B/2748